AMERICAN HERITAGE 101

A Mini Course On American Values Past, Present And Future

PAULA MATTHEWS

SL
Spirit & Life
Publications^{SM}

American Heritage 101

Copyright ©2012 Paula Matthews

Cover: Paula Matthews

All rights reserved. No part of this book may be reproduced in any form by any electronic or mechanical means including photocopying, recording, or information storage and retrieval without permission in writing from the author.

Unless otherwise noted, scripture quotations are from
The Holy Bible: Authorized King James Version,
©2003 Thomas Nelson, Inc.

Published by
Spirit & Life Publications[SM]
Los Angeles

Printed in the United States
ISBN: 978-0-9851172-6-9

The God Of Heaven
Shall Set Up A Kingdom,
Which Shall Never Be Destroyed . . . It Shall
Break In Pieces And Consume
All Other Kingdoms, And
It Shall Stand Forever.

Daniel 2:44 (Holy Bible)

Acknowledgements

In this book we will talk about spiritual heritage and I would be amiss by not taking the time to give honor to whom honor is due.

I give thanks to God for my parents, Elsie and (the late) Thomas Randles, David and (the late) Elizabeth Scott, for their prayers and support even when they never understood God's purpose for my life. They were faithful to complete their assignment in getting me into the earth for such a time as this.

A special thanks is due my spiritual parents, Apostle Frederick K.C. Price III and Dr. Betty Price for their commitment to intercede for God's will to be accomplished in my life. Their love and prayers are forever with me.

I also thank Marilyn Hickey and her team who confirmed my call to the nations at a crusade in Barcelona, Spain in 2007. My mission to Europe was halted several months later when the Lord said, *"Your Country Needs You,"* and I promptly returned to Los Angeles.

Finally, when I asked the Lord which man of God was spiritually knowledgeable about what was going on in the US, the Lord told me to call Kenneth Copeland to intercede. Thank you sir, for your obedience to the call for it was only two days later that the Lord confirmed my assignment here in the states.

In 2010, I was quietly working on the second volume ***The War Journal (1999-2010)*** when from the corner of my left eye I noticed a dark demonic force coming toward me in the spirit. Before I could think about reacting, a lightening fast laser beam came from beyond my right side and destroyed the demonic force. I immediately turned my head and noticed that the laser beam originated from the Oval Room of the White House. For years I have been covering the backs of American presidents, but this was the first time that I recall ever having an American president covering mine. From that moment to this, I have had much gratitude to God for appointing President Barack Obama and the First Lady as my ***"Spiritual Guardians"*** as I take on this assignment to the nations. I am grateful for all the prayers and words of faith you continue to speak over my life. Our country is blessed to have such a mighty team of prophetic warriors at its helm.

Finally, I thank Jesus Christ for loving humanity so much that he reconciled us back to God and restored our spiritual inheritance. Thank you Lord, for giving us your Holy Spirit and the wisdom necessary to walk this new and living way of God's Kingdom. Thank you Lord for trusting me with your anointing and call as I *make the crooked paths straight* so that your healing power can deliver the nations and prepare them for your return.

Special Dedication
To
The Late
Dr. Oral Roberts
(January 24, 1918 - December 15, 2009)

When God called me to this Kingdom assignment in 1997, I went through a miraculous spiritual transformation. For weeks at a time, I would get the sensation of fire coming from my right hand that would intensify and consume my entire arm. The Lord said it was his healing power that I would release to the nations. I was raised in the Baptist church and knew nothing about healing power except for what was in the Bible. People kept telling me that I should be laying hands and healing people, but I had no clue what that meant. I had never seen anyone lay hands on anyone.

The Lord confirmed that He anointed me to heal the multitudes with ***"His word in my mouth, and His power in my hands,"*** and it began in the strangest way. I would get into bed and as soon as my head hit the pillow, the Spirit of God would take me by the spirit to remote places in Africa and Asia. I would lay hands and minister all night long and return to my bed, worn out and barely able to speak. I asked the Lord if there was anyone to talk to about these night time excursions and he responded, **" *Yes, Oral Roberts.*"** He explained that part of my spiritual inheritance was from Dr. Roberts, and I would get a chance to talk to him about my assignment. So the Lord took me by the spirit several times to meet with Dr. Roberts in his home in Southern California. My memory of those visits is very vivid. Although I don't remember all that was said, I do remember that his lovely wife Evelyn was there because she served us drinks in glassware I had not seen since I was a kid. They were very colorful glasses, and I recall Dr. Roberts telling me that Evelyn had two variations of those glasses one was used only for iced tea, and the other only for lemonade. I don't know why, but this stands out in my mind as if we just spoke yesterday.

In 2002, the Lord had me release a limited edition of *The War Journal (1999-2010)* for leaders of the church. He also told me to write a book of the same title for public release in preparation for another attack on our nation. The Lord told me to expect a confirmation of these events from you, and in 2004 your vision *The Wake Up Call* was released to warn the church of what was about to happen in America. Thank you sir, for your faithfulness in speaking the prophetic word of God with boldness. It is because of your example that I can stand boldly in the face of death threats and much controversy to speak what God is saying to his church. I thank God for your life and ministry that has graced this earth for over ninety years. I also pray that all you have imparted to me will help me successfully accomplish every good work God has destined for my life as well.

The Lord Bringeth
The Counsel Of The Heathen To Nought:
He Maketh
The Devices Of The People Of None Effect.

The Counsel Of The LORD
Standeth For Ever,
The Thoughts Of His Heart
To All Generations.

Psalm 33:10-11

CONTENTS

SYNOPSIS 17

COURSE INTRODUCTION 21

CHAPTER 1
CONFLICTING VALUES 25
CHAPTER 2
AMERICA, THE LAWLESS 33
CHAPTER 3
NO LONGER CROWNED WITH BROTHERHOOD 39
CHAPTER 4
GOD'S KINGDOM ECONOMICS 47
CHAPTER 5
GOD REQUIRES ECONOMIC JUSTICE 55
CHAPTER 6
GOD ORDERS EQUAL TAXATION 65
CHAPTER 7
GOD'S KINGDOM AGE HAS BEGUN! 67
CHAPTER 8
NEW LEADERSHIP FOR A NEW AGE 69

CONCLUSION 73

BIBLIOGRAPHY 88

SYNOPSIS

As an author, there are times when I am haunted by a book until it is released from my spirit and appears on the written page. Such was definitely the case with ***American Heritage 101***. I had no intentions of starting a new book project while actively writing another, but it was the Spirit of God who would not leave me alone until I produced what has been showing up repeatedly in my visions and dreams.

There is a sense of urgency to this message because of the spiritual shaking that is happening in the United States and around the world. It's no coincidence that our nation is experiencing spiritual, economic and political battles simultaneously. The earth has shifted into a new spiritual dimension. God's Kingdom Age has begun and revolution is in the atmosphere. It began manifesting in the Middle East and North Africa, and according to the Spirit of God, it is about to overtake America like a *"whirlwind."* Under this new dimension, all known governmental, political and economic systems are destined to fail. The Lord also said, *"the money will fail"* in the United States. It doesn't matter what politicians propose to boost the economy, God is going to bring it down. It will fail. Biblical prophecy tells us that failure has always been God's design for the man-made economies of the earth. Daniel prophesied that God was going to raise up a Kingdom in the earth that would destroy all other earthly kingdoms. He prophesied that God's Kingdom would reign forever (Daniel 2:44).

I declare to you that God's Kingdom has already begun its operations in the earth. That is why world governments are faltering. Also, according to Bible prophecy, Jesus is going to return to earth to begin his millennial reign as King of God's Kingdom. Christians recognize the signs of Jesus' return, and expect him to break through the clouds at any minute. No! Now is not the time for Jesus to return. The earth is not ready for Jesus's return. A spiritual path of righteousness has to be prepared in the earth, to make a way for the Lord's return. That is why the Kingdom shift has begun now. If we do not prepare, Jesus could return and destroy the earth along with all its inhabitants (Malachi 4:1-6).

Consider this analogy. When the President of the United States visits another country, it is the job of the Secret Service (amongst others) to sweep the area clean of potential dangers and security concerns that could spark an international incident. Diligent intelligence and surveillance are required to "quarantine" any and all possible threats against our government and that of the host nation. This process could begin weeks, even months before the President's arrival to that nation. If a visit from the President of the United States of America could cause such a stir in a foreign nation, just think what would happen if God stepped out of Heaven and walked upon the earth.

Moses asked to see God's glory, he was told that no man could see God and live (Exodus 33:18-20). Matthew 24 gives us a preview of what it will be like when Jesus returns to earth. We won't cover the details in this book, but it would behoove the reader to take a look at the frightening scene that will be played out when Jesus comes into the earth's atmosphere. When Jesus comes back to the earth, he will come with full power and glory of God's Kingdom because he is coming to take over the earth and every eye will see it. The sun will go black and the moon will not shine. The heavens and the earth will be shaken. The inhabitants of the earth will mourn at his return. Why? The power and glory of a Holy God could destroy sinful men.

The presence of the Lord would be like a weapon of mass destruction that could take out the entire planet. We have to prepare the way for Jesus' return, so that there would be escape portals (places of refuge) to avoid the destruction that is coming to earth. This requires that we begin to seek God's Kingdom and His way of doing things now. In order to accomplish this, we must prepare hearts and minds to receive from God. His thoughts and ways are far beyond normal human comprehension, and must be spiritually discerned. This would require a complete paradigm shift for the average human being, but don't be dismayed. God in his infinite mercy has graced us with simple ways to find His way of doing things. In this book, we will attempt to simplify key spiritual concepts that can help you to begin seeing like God sees. So, let's talk about how to prepare.

When Jesus began his earthly ministry, John the Baptist was the one crying in the wilderness, prepare ye the way of the Lord (Matthew 3:3). John had to show people how to avoid that wrath of God that was coming to the earth. John said, "Repent." Which means to refrain from your current way of thinking and acting; and make a change in your life. The people asked (Luke 3:10-14), "What Shall We Do?" The answers John gave as a response are not the typical answers church folk would give if they were telling you to repent and get right with God. John didn't tell people to stop being gay, or stop killing babies, or to stop fornicating. No! He gave very simple answers that anyone could understand.

The answers John the Baptist gave spoke to our human values: how we relate to one another and how we relate to money. He told them to 1) share what they had with the poor, 2) to not cheat on taxes, 3) do violence to no man, 4) stop false accusations against each other, and 5) be content with their wages. That's all John told people to do to prepare a righteous path for God's Kingdom. John's response demonstrated a spiritual shift in man's relationship with God. Before Jesus came, religion was the only path man had to God (at least that's what men thought). Unfortunately, religion gave men laws, traditions, church rules and regulations, but no relationship with God. Religion became a god of its own and elevated itself above ordinary men in the world.

Today, Christians still serve the god of religion because they don't understand that God is a loving spiritual Father who desires a personal relationship with all men on earth. Jesus also came to show us a new way of living on earth. He gave us the commandment of love that is full of truth and an abundance of grace. Jesus commanded us to love God and to love our neighbors. He also gave us the Holy Spirit (the Spirit of Truth) who would show us how to live in this world. Being connected by love and led by spiritual truth allows us to live at peace with God and our neighbors. This is the perfect law of liberty (James 1:25) that leads us to the abundant life that God designed for all humans; his inheritance for all who come into his Kingdom. It's our wealthy place; a place of prosperity where no one suffers from lack of any good thing regardless of what may happen in the world around us.

Some may read this book and see a philosophical, even Utopian view of life. Oh, but God's Kingdom is so much more than the human mind could ever imagine. There is indeed a parallel universe in the spirit realm, and stepping out on prophetic instructions could radically change your heart, your values and your purpose for living.

So here it is. God's Kingdom is coming to rule the earth! The Age of God's Kingdom Rule has already begun to take down all religious, political and economic kingdoms of this earth. Considering this spiritual shift, how should Americans change their value systems to survive the days to come?

First, we have to change the hearts of men. America (also the church) is suffering because she desires external results over inner integrity. We tend to be shortsighted in our vision because we want quick results by any means possible. We think that legislating and adjudicating morality will change human behavior. It never works. Lawless men will always devise schemes to get around the laws of the land. Morality is not a legal issue, it's an issue of the heart, and that is where Kingdom of God begins.

Jesus said that the kingdom is within the hearts of covenant men. Jesus presented the world with a revolutionary idea; that men could change the world if they could first change their hearts to think and see like God thinks and sees. God's Kingdom does not want to destroy nations. God wants to stir men to achieve a supernatural level of greatness. Jesus said that from the good treasure of a good man's heart, he would produce good things and from the evil treasure of an evil man's heart he would produce evil things. It follows that from the Kingdom treasure of a Kingdom man's heart, he would indeed produce Kingdom of Heaven results on earth.

In this course we will explore American values, hoping to make a deposit of Kingdom treasure in the hearts of the readers. Then, they can begin to go out and produce all the good things God has stored up as an inheritance for men on earth. God is no respecter of persons. Anyone in any nation that fears God, and who will do what is right in His sight, will be accepted by him (Acts 10:34-35). We need only to Ask, Seek and Knock. It is up to each of us to find out what God would require to clear a righteous path for His return. As the nations of the world fall, those who follow God's way of doing things, will be standing in a wealthy place. This is the Will of God for Americans and for the people of the world.

COURSE INTRODUCTION

This is not a classroom course being offered by an accredited institution of higher learning. It is a series of prophetic keys of wisdom from the Spirit of God concerning American values, our "Ethos" or defining spirit that should characterize our core beliefs. Some would immediately argue that if we are discussing American ethos, why is the Christian faith being mentioned? I'm glad you asked. Since the founding of the United States, Christianity has been the underlying moral philosophy that has shaped our beliefs. The turmoil we have seen in the public square for the past fifty-plus years has been a rebellion against those founding beliefs. The reason for such rebellion is the perception that those beliefs are antiquated, and therefore have no relevancy in Modern America. This message is resonating in our judicial system, in the legislative system and in the media. The wave of terrorism is also raising a somber message that echoes around the world. People are beginning to react to religion or faith in God as something that is detrimental to society. If following God causes hatred, anger, violence and terror, why should anyone consider a life of faith? Quite simply, there is nothing wrong with a faith in God. What is wrong, is man's interpretation of what that faith means and what role it has in everyday life. This is a common struggle for every major religion.

Take Christianity for example. Men read the Bible and yet they cannot agree upon its interpretation. There are many divisions, sects or denominations. This was never God's plan. This is man's effort at interpreting what God is saying. The Bible is a spiritual book that can only be spiritually discerned. If the Spirit of God is not in you, don't expect to be able to comprehend the messages of the Bible. The Holy Spirit is our teacher, who leads us to all truth (John 16:13), and yet most Christians in America don't believe in the Holy Spirit. So, how can one speak for God without talking to God via his Spirit? This is the biggest dividing factor in Christianity. The physical proof that you belong to God is when the Holy Spirit confirms with your spirit that you are a part of God's family (Romans 8:16). Most of the church is not being led by the Spirit of God. They are being led by faulty religious doctrine and tradition. This is what we see in America. This is not true Christianity. America has yet to witness the Christianity that Jesus taught. So where have we gone wrong in America? Consider this example. Let's say that you were hired as a designer for Ford Motor Company. Your job is to build cars according to Ford's strict schematic design. What if you didn't like Ford's design and instead of going to the corporate leadership and discussing the issues, you built a design of your own? Then you go out and promote your model as something that Ford approved when it was done without their permission or knowledge. That is exactly what has happened in the Christian Church in America. They have thrown out the Bible, and have built traditions of men that cause the word of God to be of no effect. They say that their works are from God, but they serve only to promote themselves. They may even quote the Bible in support of their cause, but they don't obey that which they preach. They are hypocrites. Their desire is not to build God's Kingdom, but to exalt their own. In the process they have placed a stumbling block that keeps ordinary men from the God who sincerely desires to love and commune with them. In this course we will attempt to reverse the error that has been propagated by the American Church. We also hope to remind Americans of our rich spiritual heritage; our inheritance of freedom and prosperity that has sustained us in past generations. We want to recapture the wisdom of our founding fathers that will enable us to generate the prosperity needed for future generations.

Finally, we want to show how our nation's founding fathers designed this country from a Biblical vantage point, recognizing that those in our national family would someday include men and women of differing races, tongues and religions; like a rich dish that the French call cassoulet; where our differences are the added ingredients for a delicious experience of varying savors and textures. Jesus said that Christians are to be the salt of the earth. Americans are hooked on fast food and its high levels of sodium. So, why haven't they hooked on to Jesus who is serving up a more satisfying and healthier fare? It's simple. The church has lost its savor and is only good to be trampled under the feet of men. In this course we will look at issues that are dividing our nation along religious doctrine and political/social issues. We will show how God has designed a way for us all to prosper, if we would just obey.

This is an independent study course for those desiring to further their wisdom and understanding from God's point of view. The text contains prophecy that is indicated in bold italics. The Spirit of God speaks in plain English, simple enough for a child to understand. There is a question and answer section at the end of the course. The questions are designed to give the author's personal account of how God plans to operate in these last days. The material presented in this course should provoke the reader to continue researching on his or her own. It should be a refreshing look at our nation's challenges as we move within a new spiritual dimension.

GETTING STARTED
Before we go any further we need to establish several basic concepts that will help the reader comprehend the material in this course. This book's content has not come from human interpretation, but has been divinely downloaded to the author. We call this the *prophetic* word of God that usually comes in the form of prophecy through prayer, visions and dreams, etc. What will be discussed throughout this book is God's Kingdom prospective of what's going on in the world. You will notice that God's Kingdom prospective, the American view and that of the American Christian Church are not the same. The church in America operates without divine connection. It is a man-made institution that focuses its attention on religious doctrines and political advocacy of church ideas. God's Kingdom is benevolent in nature. It focuses more on demonstrating the power of the Blessing in the earth. The Blessing is the original mandate given to Adam for the care and maintenance of the earth and its inhabitants. It calls for the Sons of God to be fruitful and multiply the prosperous resources of the earth; to dominate and subdue the oppressors of the earth and its inhabitants. It is designed to replenish whatever was lacking in the earth. This is how the Kingdom of God was designed to operate in this earth. Unfortunately, most of the church has never known this.

When Jesus came to earth he only preached about the Kingdom. His miracles were the proof that God's Kingdom could provide whatever humans lacked on this earth. After his resurrection, Jesus continued to preach the Kingdom. He told the apostles to receive the Holy Ghost and to out to change the world with the gospel. It is resurrection power of the Holy Spirit that revives and restores any human condition in accordance to the Blessing. Jesus gave the Holy Spirit to the church and told them to go into all the world demonstrating the Kingdom (the Blessing), but they abandoned the original mandate and devised a religious way of operating in the earth. According to the Spirit of God, the moral and economic issues of America are the result of the church's abandoning the Kingdom mandate. They were called to be ambassadors of the Kingdom bringing good news of healing, deliverance and restoration to the nations of the world. They are cursing the nations rather than speaking the Blessing. The word of the Lord to the church is this: ***"My Kingdom is not like this world! Serve the nation (America) as unto God."***

Bible prophecy shows us that we are in the very last days of this world. The church has many false prophets, false teachers, and false doctrine. God's people are reluctant to hear the truth. The nations will continue to suffer, and yet God has the remedy and his people are hesitant. Consequently, God is raising up sons in the earth who are listening and who will obey His mandate to restore the nations to His original plan.

Finally, this book is based upon one spiritual assumption: **God's word is the absolute and necessary truth of God's Kingdom**. The Bible is a legal document containing decrees from the King about his Kingdom. It is also called the wisdom of God (Divine wisdom) made available to mankind. These are spiritual truths that may conflict with human facts, but when acted upon, God's word will produce the supernatural prosperity that is inherent in the Blessing. This is the inheritance that God originally designed for the nations of the earth to enjoy throughout eternity. This is why God is restoring His Kingdom upon the earth in these last days.

CHAPTER 1
CONFLICTING VALUES

THE KINGDOM PHENOMENON
"Jesus answered, My Kingdom is not an earthly kingdom." John 18:36

When one becomes a believer in Jesus Christ we are told that we are citizens of a new kingdom: God's Kingdom. God's Kingdom is a spiritual kingdom (supernatural) based upon laws far above the thoughts and ways of human beings (Isaiah 55:10). America and the nations of this world are physical (natural) kingdoms based upon laws created by the wisdom of men. God's wisdom is infinite and it never changes. Human wisdom is limited by the intellectual capabilities of men. Human wisdom is subject to change as men increase intellectually and experimentally. God is omniscient (all knowing). He knows how everything will end (Isaiah 46:10), so God's wisdom will produce the results he desired from the foundation of the world. It will yield life and not death, the Blessing not cursing. Human wisdom desires to yield life and the Blessing, but it is not possible. Abundant life is the result of men yielding to the wisdom of God. It is a gift from God to obedient men. So, when men do their own thing by following human wisdom, it always yields the curse (Jeremiah 17:5). The nature of these two kingdoms is vastly different. How is a Christian to live an earthly life in a man-made world and remain loyal to our heavenly kingdom? For many Christians this can be quite perplexing if the Holy Spirit is not leading them. One can easily be found between the Rock (Jesus) and a hard place in life.

Let's explore the Kingdom even further. Jesus told his followers not to look for a physical kingdom to appear on the earth during our lifetime. He said that the Kingdom of God is within us (Luke 17:21). How is it possible that an entire Kingdom is deposited within every believer? Well, that's where the Holy Spirit comes in. When a believer opens his heart to receive Jesus as Lord and Savior, the Holy Spirit is deposited into his or her heart. Imagine God placing within the hearts of men all the goodness, provision and prosperity of his Kingdom, then telling men to take care of the earth. Jesus demonstrated how men are no longer subject to toil to make a living as Adam did under the curse. Believers are called to live the Blessing so that we can demonstrate the power of God's Kingdom to prosper even while the world is suffering.

The Apostle Paul said that believers are called to be ambassadors reaching the world with the message of reconciliation (II Corinthians 5:17-20), and yet so many Christians are not even walking in reconciliation themselves. They suffer right along with the rest of the world while the Kingdom provision remains dormant within their hearts. They seem to have forgotten that God's Kingdom is *"solution oriented."* Jesus proved this point throughout his earthly ministry. Wherever there was sickness or disease, the Kingdom provided healing. When people were oppressed by the devil, there was deliverance. When the people were hungry, food was multiplied to feed them all. The lame walked and the blind had their sight restored. The captives were set free. These are works of God's Kingdom. The prophet Isaiah described the works of God's Kingdom by saying God will give you beauty for ashes; a garment of praise for the spirit of heaviness. He said that for our shame, God would give us double reward; instead of disgrace God would give rejoicing (Isaiah 61:1-3,7). This is the replenishing and restoring power that America and the world so desperately needs.

It is the Holy Spirit who imparts to believers the power to overcome every obstacle in this life. He is our source for every thing that needs replenishing on earth. This is part of our inheritance as children of God, and yet so many Christians live like orphan children separated from God. What a disgrace to God's Kingdom, when his children are walking in the fear of making a living when their father has set aside more than enough for them to live in abundance for an eternity. Jesus told his followers not to worry about how to make a living like the rest of the world. He told them to seek first the Kingdom of God and his righteousness and all these things will be added unto you (Matthew 6:31-33), but so many Christians simply don't believe this is true. Many think that the Kingdom of God is only operational in Heaven. That is not what Jesus taught. He said the Kingdom of God was within us and he demonstrated the power of the Kingdom with every miracle.

The greatest sign of the Kingdom, was when Jesus was crucified, buried and resurrected from the dead. He proved that the Kingdom of God has power even over death. It is by this one miracle that one must confess belief in the lordship of Jesus Christ. Romans 10:9 says that if we confess with our mouths the lordship of Jesus and believe in our hearts that God raised him from the dead, then we would be saved. Many Christians confess with their mouths, but in their hearts they don't believe. If

God could do all those miracles through Jesus and then raise him from the dead, he could do the same for, and through anyone who believes. The same spirit that did miracles through Jesus; the same spirit that raised him from the dead is the same Holy Spirit that is given to every believer so that they can do the same thing on earth (Romans 8:11). There is no need to fear our living or death.

KINGDOM AMBASSADORS ON EARTH
" . . . And these signs shall follow them that believe" Mark 16:17

The Spirit of God is grieved because many Christians are under the false assumption that miracles only follow great men of God or great ministries. The word clearly says that miraculous signs would follow anyone who believes. So, if you are a Christian, are the miraculous signs of Jesus Christ following you? If not, I would question if you are truly a believer. Our commission from God is clear. We are to go into the entire world preaching the Gospel and teaching what Jesus taught. Does this mean that you hold up a Bible and start preaching at your place of employment? Not necessarily. But it does mean that your conduct and lifestyle should represent the interest of God's Kingdom. Ambassadors represent their home country on foreign soil. An ambassador's job is to educate those of the host nation about the ways of his or her home country. It's the highest-ranking Public Relations representative of that country. The ambassador is also expected to develop key economic, cultural and scientific relationships between the two nations.

So, I ask you, fellow Christian and Ambassador Elect, how are you representing God's Kingdom where he has sent you? He appointed you at an employer. Have you offered suggestions that God gave you to improve that business' operations? If not, what are you waiting for? He has appointed you to a particular family, in a particular city, state and community. What has God given you to implement that will greatly benefit that family, or city, state or community? God has appointed you to a particular school or university system. As they educate you on their ways, have you informed them on God's Kingdom ways as well?

Remember, you are an ambassador. If you say he has given you nothing, I question whether you are communicating with the home nation at all. God is always communicating, why aren't you listening? Wherever God appoints his people, his plan is to create change; to bring healing where is there is suffering and pain; to bring freedom where there is oppression; to create peace where there is war; to turn every devastation and ruin into prosperity. So, if you are in a situation that is suffering, it is God's plan for you as his ambassador to seek him for answers on how to turn things around. I don't care if you are the President of the United States or the janitor for the poorest company in America. The power to change the environment from devastation to prosperity is in your hands. It's not about you. It's about a God who so desperately wants to put an end to human suffering. God gave us dominion. He can only intervene if his people on earth are willing and obedient. I urge each of you who claim to be a believer in Jesus Christ to obey God. The dreams and plans he gave you are for a specific time and purpose; and that time is now. When you obey God, you glorify him in the earth. It shows that you believe him and not the circumstances of this world.

THE MYOPIC CHRISTIAN VIEW

"They are demanding that the nation obey God and yet Christians don't obey him . . ." Prophecy from July 15, 2012 *"Who is Lord and Master of Your Life?"*

The Spirit of God has had me praying for the deliverance of Christians in America. He said that they have a *"myopic view of the world."* There is a widespread lack of understanding about how God and his Kingdom operate. To make matters worse, American Christians tend to juxtapose the Kingdom of God with that of the US Government. This has resulted in compromised allegiances. America is a republic with people of many religions and creeds. The Kingdom of God is both a theocracy and monarchy where Jesus is King, and all the people have one faith, one baptism, one God and Father of all. American Christians tend to treat God's Kingdom like a government run by democracy; and they treat America like a kingdom with one faith and one God. They don't want God to be their Lord and Master, but yet they want America to submit to God as Lord and Master. This is both a perverted and hypocritical ideology that is widely supported in most religious circles. They can see the toothpick in someone else's eye, but they can't see the plank in their own (Matthew 7:5). These Christians fast and pray to put others into bondage under the Bible because they don't understand the spirit of truth on which the Bible was written. They think they know all there is to know about God, and yet Psalm 147:5 says that God's wisdom and understanding is infinite. Christians tend to forget that God has a special grace for those who don't know him, and that they too are partakers of that same grace of God.

So what should Christians be doing in this hour? Every believer should be taking heed to the words of Isaiah 58 and then turning their hearts back to God. This passage describes a people who religiously fast and pray. God does not answer them because they fast and pray to achieve wicked results, results that are against the will and Kingdom of God. Their sacrifices are in vain. God ordains us to pray and fast to release people from oppression. In this hour we should be releasing people in our nation by taking care of the poor, the hungry and the wounded. We should seek the will of God and cease from doing our own thing, especially on the Sabbath.

If we do all these things then God will cause our righteousness to shine as a bright light in the darkness of this world. It's our obedience that causes God's light to shine. If American Christians would begin to live according God's will, then we would see a great change in our nation. Then all men would see the light of God's glory and turn their hearts to him.

CHRISTIAN POLITICS: TO CONDEMN OR TO SAVE THE WORLD

"God sent his son not to condemn the world, but that the world through him might be saved." John 3:17

In a vision of horror, I saw several prominent leaders of the Christian church plummet onto a slippery slope, which landed them in Hell. These men were convinced that joining a political campaign to support a pro family agenda was the will of God. The Spirit of God spoke a truth that rang loudly in my spirit. He said that the pro family agenda was not pro family at all. It is a deliberate attempt to sway the hearts of weak-minded voters to join a movement that is full of hate and deception. He said that the pro family agenda is a smoke screen for a carefully crafted **"Anti-Gay"** agenda, and for the church or its leaders to join in such hateful rhetoric is the same as condemning all gays to Hell. The Lord said that Christians should be praying for HIS WILL and not affirming the will of a political agenda. To do otherwise is to go against God's Kingdom which commands all Christians to Go Into All the World not to condemn the world, but to "Evangelize" the world.

Christians are called to demonstrate the love of God and to live peaceable with all men. We should be displaying good works of the Kingdom that would cause all men to glorify our Father in Heaven and to desire him as their God. Taking a political stand against any people group is to cause an even wider chasm between the world and God. Jesus died for all men. God sent Jesus not to condemn the world, but to save the world. So as Followers of Jesus Christ, who are we to condemn anyone? Dear Christians do you not know that you were given the ministry of reconciling the world back to God? Before you condemn gays or those who have had abortions, take a look around the Body of Christ. They are among us. They are us . . . our brothers and sisters who are seeking the love of God and secretly living in condemnation, not because God has condemned them, but you, the Church have condemned them. If condemning the world is against the plan and purpose of God, how much more is condemning those among the brethren? How dare you place a stumbling block in the paths of those who are seeking the love of God! Jesus said that it would be better for you if a millstone were placed on your neck and you be drowned in the sea!

God is saying to His People, ***"Babylon is falling! Come out of her my people! Lest you be partakers in her sins and receive her judgments and plagues."*** Repent. Change your mind and your behavior. Make your words, actions and deeds consistent with God and his purpose for all men: which is that they be saved and to come to the knowledge of the truth of his love for them.

THE DEFIANT BABYLONIAN CHURCH
IN AMERICA

Many a Christian leader in America has been heard complaining about the Babylonian system of operation that has plagued our country for generations. If you ask God what's wrong with the American Christian Church, he would give you the same answer: its Babylonian system of operation. The Spirit of God explained that America as a whole, operates under the Babylonian rebellion because of the Church's rebellion against God. Here's an excerpt ***The War Journal (1999-2010) Volume II***: *"The Word of the Lord came to me saying; "This is the American Church." And then I saw a beautifully formed, powerful physical structure in the form of a man. Atop the body was a handsome strong head; but what I saw next startled me. As the body moved, it did so without the head. There were no lacerations, no broken skin fragments about the neck. It was then that I realized; the body and head were never connected! The Lord said that the Body of Christ in America was in agreement with its members. The Church was built in the similitude of the Tower* *of Babel."* It was in Babel that the people were in agreement to make a tower that would reach to Heaven so that the people could make a name for themselves (Genesis 11:1-9). It was as though they were saying as Lucifer said in Isaiah 14:14; *"I will ascend above the clouds; and I will be like the Most High God."* When Lucifer spoke these words; God cast him out of Heaven and exiled him to earth. When the people of Babel decided they could reach Heaven without God. He came to earth and confused their language and scattered them across the face of the earth.

The Spirit of God compared the Church in America to the Tower of Babel. Noah's sons were commanded to go and replenish the earth after the flood. Instead of obeying God they decided to dwell in a plain in the land of Shinar. That is where they were determined to build a monument to themselves. Likewise, the Church was commanded to go into the world and teach all nations in order to repair and replenish the earth. Instead they have chosen to stay in their local communities and build an organizational structure to appease God. Traditions of men and the agenda of the Church are given the highest priority over anything that God has commanded in the Bible. With both the Tower Babel and the American Church, men created their own sense of righteousness and decided that they could reach Heaven without God. These structures were religiously built to glorify the works of men on the earth.

When God scattered the builders of the tower, men were sent to the utter most parts of the earth, just as God had planned from the beginning (Genesis 10:5, 20, 31-32). Likewise, the American Church will also be scattered and God will raise up the sons of God (His church) who will go across the world teaching, healing, replenishing and repairing those who have been oppressed by the devil, just as God had planned from the beginning. God will again prove that the collective genius of men is no match for the divine providence of God. If God said it; he will surely bring it to pass, no matter what men agree to do amongst themselves.

CHAPTER 2

AMERICA, THE LAWLESS

The United States of America is notably a great nation in many ways; but the spirit that drives us to achieve greatness is the same spirit that causes us to become arrogant, prideful and self-indulgent in a manner that is counterproductive and offensive. Because we have done so many great things, we believe that rules of order no longer apply. Americans believe that, "we make the rules." We act like gifted children who have a false sense of entitlement. Americans idolize their ability to control and manipulate people and circumstances to suit their needs. That's why we can elect officials that say what we want them to say, but when he or she tries to do what is best for us, we threaten to fire them and elect someone else. Some might say this is how the democratic process works, but there a deeper issue at stake. On the world's stage, we have lost our edge because, we don't want to be right, we want to be popular. We've lost our sense of right and wrong. This is evident in our media, in politics, business and especially in the Christian church where the spiritual prima donnas think they are above God's law. We will see in this chapter how this spirit of entitlement has been our nation's flaw from the very beginning.

IS AMERICA REALLY A CHRISTIAN NATION?

"In The Name of God, Amen. We whose names are underwritten, the loyal subjects of our Dread Sovereign Lord King James, by the Grace of God of Great Britain, France, and Ireland, King Defender of the Faith, etc. Having Undertaken, For the Glory of God And Advancement of the Christian Faith And Honor of our King and Country, A Voyage to Plant the First Colony in the Northern Parts of Virginia, Do by These Presents Solemnly and Mutually In the Presence of God and One of Another, Covenant and Combine ourselves together into a Civil Body Politic . . ." Translated Excerpt of the Mayflower Compact of 1620.[1]

When the Puritans landed in New World in the 1600's, they were escaping the tyrannical rule of King James and the Church of England. It was their desire to establish a new settlement in which they could live as God prescribed in the Bible. The Puritans believed in the literal interpretation of the Bible. King James believed that it was the divine right of kings to interpret the Bible anyway they choose, and the loyal subjects would be required to obey under threats of imprisonment or death. After all, it was illegal for commoners to possess the Bible, so how could they argue with their lord and king? Yet, that is exactly what many of the Puritans did. The decision to flee from England was a dangerous one, but the Puritans risked everything in search of their "Promised Land." Some even referred to the New World as the "New Jerusalem." They believed that it was God's divine providence that led them here and they created the Mayflower Compact to validate the reason for their establishment of the colonies. The Mayflower Compact was written and signed before the ship landed in the new land. This was a brief review of our nation's founding. It used to be taught in grade school, but so many people have tried to erase America's Christian roots, that this information has been lost to recent generations. So, here is your pop quiz. *Given how the colonies were first established: Is America a Christian Nation?* The Spirit of God says, *"NO!"* He said that America is a country made up of many Christians, but we are not a Christian nation.

Now, many Christian leaders would disagree this answer, but the Lord took me back through history and I will share what I have learned. America had the chance to become a Christian nation, but the early settlers could not agree upon doctrine. In general, no one debated whether or not he or she believed in the Bible, but the question was how to govern a nation in accordance with Biblical law. The Puritans were the most successful at Biblical governance. In fact, some of those laws still exist on the books today. Blue "rigidly moral" Laws are still used in many states regarding keeping the Sabbath day holy. It used to be that few, if any businesses would be open on Sunday, but now many states just restrict certain business activities on that day.

Now let's go back to the Puritans. The colonies began to polarize according to their differing Christian beliefs, which resulted in each state establishing its own church, and the laws of these states were designed to reflect the religious beliefs of the people. For example, if you were in an Anglican State you could be jailed for preaching Jesus according to Baptist doctrine. The Danbury Baptist Association wrote a letter to President Thomas Jefferson appealing for help in addressing this issue. Thomas Jefferson wrote a response letter that has since been misconstrued to justify the notion of "separation of church and state." Our courts say that Jefferson's intent was for there to be a separation between church and state, and yet the Library of Congress has documented evidence that Jefferson attended church every Sunday. And here is the kicker, the church services were being held in the House of Representatives. In fact there is proof that throughout his administration Jefferson approved of church services being held in the executive branch offices even in the chambers of the Supreme Court. The Library of Congress has this information documented in the section of the exhibit entitled **Religion and the Founding of the American Republic, VI. Religion and the Federal Government (Part 2),** "The State Becomes the Church: Jefferson and Madison."[2] Hold on to your hat because there is more.

Here is a direct quote from this Library of Congress exhibit: *"Jefferson's actions may seem surprising because his attitude toward the relation between religion and government is usually thought to have been embodied in his recommendation that there exist 'a wall of separation between church and state.' In that statement, Jefferson was apparently declaring his opposition, as Madison had done in introducing the Bill of Rights, to a 'national' religion. In attending church services on public property, Jefferson and Madison consciously and deliberately were offering symbolic support to religion as a prop for republican government."*

FYI. This exhibit was not put together by any religious or Christian ministerial organization. It was a done by the Library of Congress staff and the exhibition was made possible by grants from The Pew Charitable Trusts, Mr. and Mrs. Henry J. (Bud) Smith, and the Lilly Endowment Inc. The national tour of the exhibition was made possible by the Lilly Endowment Inc.

Now that I have your full attention, I want to share one final astounding note about this exhibit. The Library of Congress has copies of the original ideas for our national seal (**See Religion and the Founding of the American Republic 1777-89, IV. Religion and the Congress of the Confederation, "Proposed Seal for the United States."**)[3] Benjamin Franklin wanted the Biblical story of the parting of the Red Sea. Jefferson proposed as our official national seal, the story of The Children of Israel, led by a Cloud by Day and a Pillar of Fire by night. Does this sound like our founders wanted a wall of separation between church and state? No! So, tell me, what kind of nation would allow it's judicial system to slander the religious views of our founding fathers by issuing decrees based upon erroneous legal and faulty interpretations? Think about it! **Now ask yourself this question:** *Is America a Christian Nation?*

Let's move on. The Puritans weren't the only settlers on this new land. Many others came looking for ways to make material wealth. Although they may have claimed to be Christian, when it came right down to it, these other settlers served the Almighty Dollar and they despised Almighty God. Their lust for wealth caused them to kill Native Americans in order to steal their land. The natives who survived were then either corralled like animals onto government reservations while others were shipped off to special schools where they would be taught to forgo their "savage ways" in order that they might adopt the white man's "civilized ways." America's early settlers also transported multiplied millions of human beings from Africa who were chained together like animals and brought to this country to be used as slaves. They degraded a race of people who were descendants of great wealth and mighty kings. In ***The War Journal (1999-2010) Volume II***, I wrote about how we illegally acquired Hawaii. Christian missionaries settled on the island to teach Jesus. They did such a good job of proselytizing, that the Hawaiian people changed their national motto to reflect their newly adopted Christian lifestyles. Those same missionary families organized a military coup and overthrew Hawaii's reigning family, in addition to killing many of its people. In 1993, President Bill Clinton signed Public Bill 103-150 as an apology to the Hawaiian people for the illegal overthrow of their monarchy.[4] We owe more than an apology to the Indians, the Africans, the Hawaiians, and all other people we have destroyed in order to build this nation. What is heartbreaking is that this was the pattern early American's established. We taught them about Jesus while we plotted to abuse them, kill them and rape and pillage their lands.

There is a preponderance of documented proof that our founding fathers believed in the Bible. It's in our archives, in our museums, on our celebrated monuments and civic buildings. Doesn't this prove something? **For the final time I will ask you:** *Is America a Christian Nation?* The Holy Spirit said, *"No!"* *"One is not a Christian because they can read the scriptures and place them on official documents and upon the walls of buildings. That makes one simply a hearer of the word. The one, who does the word, who treats his neighbor with* *love is truly Christian. They are more than a hearer; they are a doer of God's word. The same is true for any nation who desires to be considered a Christian Nation."* According to history, neither Jefferson nor many of the founders opposed a firm Biblical foundation for our nation. There's no denying the wealth of documented information about our Christian roots, but one question remains: *Why Didn't Our Founding Fathers Openly Declare This Nation as a Christian Nation?* Could it be as the Library of Congress concluded in the discussion about the wall of separation between church and state? Our founders just didn't want to declare a "national religion." Consider this. Puritan Law, in many ways was just as brutal as Sharia Law in Islamic countries. People were stoned to death and burned in the public square for violating religious ordinances. How can you enforce strict Biblical doctrinal laws upon Jews, Catholics, Quakers or other faiths? And yet, this is exactly what happened in the colonial states. People were imprisoned and lost their lives because their religious views were different from those espoused by the state in which they had settled. Is this not the reason that the Puritans fled England? How unfortunate it would have been for those who had been oppressed under the strict religious ruler ship of their King, to take refuge in a new land only to establish a nation that practiced the same religious tyranny. Clearly it was the foresight of our founding fathers to direct us in the best way they knew how to establish a nation: upon the fundamental moral law of the Bible; while leaving us the freedom of choice in how we worship. They led us to the Living Waters, but they did not force us to drink from the same well. Unfortunately, the embodiment of the modern Christian Church in America still holds to the tyrannical rule that oppresses the people, and God is about to tear that system down.

For all the reasons stated above, America's chance of becoming a Christian nation is a *"missed opportunity,"* but we do have one *"ace in the hole"* according to God. He reminded me that he always honors those who honor him, and when the Puritans came to our shores they did so to honor God. They solidified this honor by making a covenant with Almighty God when they created the Mayflower Compact of 1620. Once a covenant is made with God, it can never be broken, and herein lies a blessing. A covenant with the Almighty ensures that whenever our nation or its people are in trouble, or in dire need of anything, if we will only turn our hearts to him (regardless of our religious beliefs), he will remember the covenant, hear our prayers and heal our land.

AMERICA AT WAR WITH GOD

A noted prophetic Christian teacher and pastor recently reported that many of the Church's prophets are prophesying war and doom for America. This pastor and his congregation are determined to see that these prophecies are just rumors of war. Rather than jumping on the bandwagon of the doomsday prophets, the people of faith are fasting and praying for our nation. God has declared a prosperous end for America. We believe that no matter what comes against us here in America; God has a plan for good and not for evil. Are these prophets wrong? Yes . . . and No. Matthew Chapter 24 is very specific about the evil times that lie ahead for the world. America is not exempt from the wars and rumors of wars; or the famines, earthquakes and tumults of the end times; but Jesus was very clear in telling believers NOT TO FEAR!

This is the Year of Increase. God has a plan to do us good. If you obey the plan of God and remain faithful to his plan, then when terror comes you will see it but it won't touch you (Psalm 91:1-9). In ***The War Journal (1999-2010) Volume I*** it states that war is indeed coming to America, but God will use it as a platform to prosper those who will follow him. According to this book, the war has already begun; it began in the hearts of men who want power over our country; men in politics; men in religious factions; men in business; men whose hearts lust for power and control over a nation whose destiny has been sealed in the purpose of God. As these men war and lust against each other, they war against the God who chose America and sealed her destiny In Him. ***"America is at war with God. Unless Christian leaders bow their knees to the Lord they claim to follow; and actually obey his will, the conditions for armed conflict will escalate. Unless politicians lay aside their political agendas and honor God so that we all may live peaceable in this nation, tensions will continue to escalate. Conditions for war are escalating because Christians in America have turned their hearts away from God in order to do their own thing; BUT when God's People who are called by His Name; humble themselves and pray and seek His Face and turn from their wicked ways; Then will God hear from Heaven; forgive our sins and He Will Heal Our Land."***

CHAPTER 3

NO LONGER CROWNED WITH BROTHERHOOD

There was a time in America that we were our brother's keeper. We even watched out for each other's children. Remember when parents, teachers and the church all worked together to raise the neighborhood children? We seemed to understand that if one of us suffered, then the entire community suffered; but something happened to America. We separated from our neighbors because they have different beliefs. Now we label people by their actions, and then categorize them as either good or bad. It's bad enough when the media or politicians call each other liberals or conservatives, socialists or communists, but it's another thing when the Christian church does the same thing. In fact, the church is worse than the world because they create divisions based upon such things as denomination, financial and/or marital status, sex, culture and race.

God made only one race: the human race. The Bible says that God created all nations of men from one blood (Acts 17:26). In the eyes of God there is no difference between Jew, Christian, unbelievers or those who believe nothing at all. The truth is we are all struggling in this human experience to find the way to love, prosperity and purpose. Our methods of discovery are different, but our desires are the same because God designed us that way. Jesus is still appointed as the Lord of all men; and he is willing to richly bless all who will come to him (Romans 10:12-13). The Holy Spirit says that the church is **"Hung up on Religion; but the Kingdom is now about One New Man (the Body of Christ)."**

In this chapter we will take a look at how the worldview clashes with religion, but God's Kingdom view settles the difference.

HOUSE RULES
Christians are called to be followers of Jesus Christ. He is our example for living and loving God and man. We do so with the wisdom of God, along with grace and truth. In his ministry, Jesus revealed practical truths about God's desired relationship with men. Jesus came demonstrating the Grace of God when he revealed the heart and mind of God in dealing with the human condition of sin. Many Christians have been beaten down by religion. Consequently, they know nothing about the love or mercy of God. Jesus taught about God as a loving father who wants the

best for his children. Every parent has HOUSE RULES that the family must follow. These rules cannot be applied to someone else's house unless one chooses to apply them. Visitors to your house must follow the HOUSE RULES, but if they choose not to obey, they can simply go home. No one will force them to obey OUR HOUSE RULES. That is how God looks at sin. Sinners are outside of God's house; but once you join God's family you are required to follow GOD'S HOUSE RULES. To use or conspire to use the BIBLE (GOD'S HOUSE RULES) to stone and condemn a sinner is WRONG! It is a clear form of oppression. Oppression occurs when one enslaves another either by great physical force or by overwhelming entanglements that bind another person to the point that they are unable to achieve positive results and unable to escape negative consequences.

This is like stoning the blind man and condemning him to death because he cannot see. Of course he cannot see he is blind. Telling him that he is blind will not open his eyes to make him see. Only the Power of God through the Holy Spirit can open blind eyes. It is also the only power that will make sinners turn away from sin. So, when dealing with homosexuality, gay marriage, or any perceived sin we must see as God sees. This can only be done if we are listening to the Holy Spirit. Unfortunately too many Christians have treated gays with hatred because they were only looking at the Law, not at the heart of God. God is love and Jesus is the truth, and because of what many Christians have done, the paths to both truth and love have been blocked for gay people. This was never God's plan.

For the record, all men sin. They may not be gay or in any sexual sin, but all men sin. So get off the backs of gay people. Christians are very quick to call someone a sinner but John 16:8 says that it is the job of the Holy Spirit to convict the world of sin. He convicts them and then draws them to God. Jesus said that no one can come to him unless the Father draws them. So, yelling at someone and calling him or her a sinner will not draw them to God; it only drives them further away.

LET HIM WHO HAS NO SIN
CAST THE FIRST STONE
The court ruling against Prop 8 caused quite a stir around the world. Although the voters in California voiced their opinion about gay marriage, the 9th Circuit Court of Appeals determined that Prop 8 was unconsti-

tutional. This was a hot political topic that would have lasting repercussions. Many Christians would say this ruling is an affront to the laws of God as stated in the Bible; and yes they would be right. But, there is a bigger issue at stake. How far will Americans go to violate another person's rights based on a religious view? Jesus had a similar situation when the religious leaders brought to him a woman caught in the act of adultery (John 8:1-11). The Spirit of God says that what is happening to gays in America is similar to what happened to this adulterous woman.

Book Excerpt:

"Even the issues with homosexuality are on the rise because of their prevalence in the church. The Spirit of God simply says to the church; "Let him who has no sin cast the first stone at the gays." This is what Jesus told the religious leaders of his day who brought to him a woman that was caught in the act of adultery. Jesus died so that we can be exonerated of our sins. So, if you have committed sexual sin or any other kind of sin against God, just ask him to forgive you. Then do as Jesus said to that woman accused of adultery; "Go and sin no more." Sexual issues are not political; they are spiritual in nature. By making political propaganda out of these issues the church is shirking its responsibility. At a time when so many church leaders are complaining about "BIG GOVERNMENT" interfering in the lives of its citizens, why add to the government's responsibility that which God gave to the church? Morality should be taught in the church and reinforced in the home. Forcing the government to legislate moral issues is ludicrous. If the Laws of Moses could not keep people from sinning against God; what makes Christians think that the laws of the United States would do any better?" Issue of Conflict: Our Social Disgrace, ***The War Journal (1999-2010) Volume II*** by Paula Matthews.

IS GAY MARRIAGE A SIN?

Not only has gay marriage been the subject of public debate for the past several years, but it was also weighing heavy upon the heart of God as well. On April 12th of 2012, I created a podcast entitled *"The Spirit of Babylon Manifested in Marriage,"* we briefly discussed gay marriage as one of the many ways in which most marriages have strayed from God's grand design. While praying about the subject for this podcast, the Spirit of God dropped a question in my spirit: ***"Is Gay Marriage a Sin?"*** For days, the main conversation God spoke to me about was gay marriage.

The answer to this question comes straight from the heart of God. It is full of his grace, wisdom and compassion. The Spirit of God said that yes, he does have laws against homosexuality and all sexual sin. God said that he also has a specific design and purpose for marriage that he also expects us to follow. Then he said something that really hit home with me. The Spirit of God said, *"Yes these things are true"* but he also has a **"SPECIAL GRACE for those who don't know him or know of his ways."** The grace of God is the mercy and loving kindness of God. It is the goodwill and favor of God. It is the supernatural empowerment that God extends to humans on the earth. The grace of God flows out of his endless love and compassion towards all men . . . regardless of how we treat God . . . regardless of whether or not we obey him. Now, the more we love and obey God, the more grace he give us; but God's grace is extended to all men. Grace is when God shows leniency towards us and either lets us off or gives us much less than what we deserve when we sin against him. So, before you judge another person's sin, take a look at your own.

Most Christians claim not to committee the obvious sins but consider the following. When was the last time you looked at a man or a woman and lusted? Have you ever cheated on your taxes . . . or lied about your age, your weight or you natural hair or its color? Have you ever lied, or stretched the truth on your resume . . . lied about another person or on another person? Have you stolen money or supplies from a friend or an employer or family member? Have you ever cheated on a test? Have you ever lied or withheld the truth from someone to protect yourself? Have you cheated on your husband or wife? Have you slept with someone while you were single? Have you ever killed anyone . . . thought about killing someone . . . or spoken about killing someone? Have you ever strongly desired something that someone else had; like a job, a car, a home or his or her spouse? Have you ever cursed or disrespected your father or mother? Or spoken evil or conspired to speak evil against another person including your spouse, your employer, even a celebrity or political figure? Have you ever broken your word or a covenant? Is God first in your life? Have you ever falsely accused someone . . . or plotted against them?

If you have answered yes beware, God considers all these actions a sin. Again, God knows what is in your heart. So while you may have judged gay marriage as a sin. Take a look at your own life? For the believer whatever is not done in faith is considered sin. So judge your own lives first and you will see that we have all fallen short of what God desires. In the eyes of God, sin is sin. Period.

THE ABORTION DECEPTION
I was awaken with a sense of sadness as I listened to the Lord talk about how his people have been deceived about abortion. Just because abortion is legal, women don't have to make that choice. Unfortunately many are making that choice because others are forcing it upon them. In America we call it a woman's right to choose, but a closer look at the issue shows that most women get abortions because they feel they have no other choice. For the underage girl, her parents are making the choice for her. For the woman trapped in an extramarital affair, the man wanting to protect his image is making the choice for her. The single career woman whose pregnancy could mean the loss of a job or promotion, or even loss of esteem among her peers, abortion seems like the only choice. Even the single women active in the church who stumbled and fell. Unwilling to carry the shame of a public pregnancy, she made a choice for abortion. She felt there was no other choice. None of these women are really making the choice because they want to, but because abortion is being forced upon them by the actions and opinions of others. This is no different from the prostitute or sex worker who is being forced against her will to have an abortion so that her pregnancy will not interrupt the flow of her money making ability.

Historically speaking, women have always been told that they had the choice of what to do with their bodies, but in actuality the choice is being made for them. Abortion is just another smokescreen for those who are on the side of abusing women and families. Why doesn't anyone stop this abuse of women? Why should a woman be mutilated because she wants to remain in a relationship with someone, or wants to keep her position in life? Why is birth control a woman's issue and abortion a woman's choice? Abortion reduces women to nothing more than a sexual utensil. Something to be used, abused and thrown away when finished and the men walk about unscathed.

According to the Spirit of God abortion is not a political issue. It is a deeper issue of morality that expresses the lack of value of women and children in our society. It also works in direct opposition to God's plan for mankind. For every child that is conceived in the earth, God has a plan and purpose. It's not just any purpose, but one that holds the key to the resources and ingenuity necessary for human kind to survive. The nations of the world are suffering for lack of knowledge of how to solve our problems. We must stop and ask, how many of those aborted babies were given the keys to that knowledge? The solutions have been denied the light of day because someone chose to end a life? How many Einsteins have we lost? How many were given the cure for cancer and other widespread diseases? God creates everyone and everything for a purpose, but abortion causes us to cut off our nose to spite our face. Voting at the ballot box will not solve this problem. Only fervent prayer and a miracle from God will bring America back to her right mind.

THE TRUE MINISTRY OF JESUS CHRIST RESTORES HONOR TO WOMEN

"Now, when Jesus was risen . . . he appeared first to Mary Magdalene"
Mark 16:9

Did you ever wonder why Jesus chose to first show himself to a woman after his resurrection? I asked that question of God and he responded by saying that **"Jesus restored honor to women."** The Lord then reminded me of Jesus' ministry on earth and how his most dedicated followers were women, and why not? Jesus stood up for the rights of women in an environment where women were held in little or no esteem. Oppression of women was a serious issue in Jesus' day, as it is in ours. God has always hated divorce (still does). In that day men were allowed to have their wives killed if it was suspected that she was an adulteress. Therefore, some men began falsely accusing their wives, just so they could kill one and marry another woman. So, Moses allowed men to divorce their wives as an alternative to killing them (Matthew 19:3-10).

Women were so reviled, that it was not allowed for men to speak to women in public, and yet Jesus spoke with the woman at the well, and healed her from a life of fornication and adultery (John 4:4-30). A woman during her menstrual cycle was considered so unclean, that she had to separate herself from society; and yet when the woman with the issue of blood for twelve years pressed through a crowd to touch the hem of Jesus' robe; she was immediately healed. The doctors took all her money and left her diseased and disgraced, but Jesus acknowledged her faith, her healing, and returned her to wholeness in the midst of the crowd (Luke 8:40-48). Even when the religious leaders tried to get Jesus to agree to sentencing to death the woman caught in the act of adultery;

Jesus publicly defended the woman, not because she was innocent, but because the leaders set the woman up in order to twist the Law of Moses. According to the Law, if a couple was caught in adultery, both the man and the woman were to be stoned. The religious leaders brought no man, only a woman to be judged (John 8:1-11). Whether it is the act of exploiting women in the sex trade industry, or in pornography, or verbal abuse and misuse in the church and family; if Jesus were walking our streets today, he would be outspoken about the treatment of both women and children in our world. He would show us how to love the person inspite of their sin.

A WOMAN'S RIGHT TO CHOOSE
DEATH AND THE CURSE

"My people are destroyed because of a lack of knowledge . . . because you have rejected knowledge . . . I (God) will also forget your children." Hosea 4:6

We spoke about how Jesus returned honor to women, and while writing that section the Spirit of God began talking about how women in this world have been deceived into bringing dishonor upon themselves in the act of abortion. This is not a political message, but a spiritual one that God spoke to my heart, a message that is specifically for those who call themselves Christians. Why Christians? Many of the women getting abortions in America today are women in the church. So many women in the church use abortion as a means of birth control, and if they clearly understood how God looks at not only abortion, but also the entire act of sex outside of marriage, they would change their ways. While church leaders are clamoring about abortion laws, they totally miss the point. Just because abortion is legal doesn't mean a woman has to make that choice. Many make that choice because the church is not doing its job of teaching that a Christian's body is the temple of God. Few people would find it enticing to have sex, and then commit murder in the sanctuary of a church, and yet that is what abortion is doing to those who call themselves children of God.

Fellow believer, we cannot do with our bodies what we want. Jesus bought us with his precious blood. We are no longer our own. As Christians, we are covenanted with God and his son, and have become members of His Body. So, what we do to our bodies, we do to the Body of Christ. As believers we are commanded to be fruitful and multiply. This is our blessing from God. Children are a gift from God and the fruit of the womb is considered a blessing (Psalm 127:3), but when it is aborted this is considered a curse. When God made his covenant with Noah, he also made a provision against shedding the blood of another human being. Whoever takes the life of a human will have his or her life taken by a human. The curse brings death. Confess and repent for taking a life, then the Blood of Jesus will cleanse you and God will restore you in right standing (I John 1:9). Forgive yourself and move on. Take this truth you have received and pass it on to others in the faith. Keep in mind that we must all appear at the judgment seat to give an account to God everything we have done in these bodies; both good and bad (II Corinthians 5:10).

Finally, the Spirit of God had commentary on the vilification of Planned Parenthood. He said *"The organization is providing a vital service to the public. Yes, there are abortions, but has anyone asked why they are doing it? Shut them down, then you need to shut down Stem Cell Researchers who are buying fetuses from young women like people sell blood plasma. It's bigger than Planned Parenthood. Embryonic stem cells have yielded no results nor will they ever," says God. "Adult stem cells hold the clues to life."*

Supplemental Reading: For more about abortion, read the Ezine Article entitled, *"Abortion: The Death of God's Seed"* by Paula Matthews, (http://ezinearticles.com/6707687).

To learn more about what God's Kingdom requires in our relationships with men and with God, Read *The Sermon on the Mount* (Matthew Chapters 5,6,7). This is the Kingdom Manifesto. It tells what is required to be blessed in the Kingdom. It deals with issues such as divorce, anger, adultery and dealing with enemies.

CHAPTER 4

GOD'S KINGDOM ECONOMICS

SEEK THE KINGDOM; NOT A JOB
The "American Dream" defines success by what one possesses in life: a good education and a good job; a lovely home, impressive car; a beautiful wife with two or three children and a dog. In our distant past, this was a good thing because people took pride in their work and their ability to provide the best for their families, community and nation. Being an American meant striving to be the best you could be. We were a God fearing nation that cared for our families and neighbors the best that we could. We were loyal to our nation, our employers and our family. Although we had issues as a nation, we attempted to remain cohesive because there were bigger enemies outside of our borders that threatened our liberty. Then there was an age of disillusionment in which we saw our nation's leaders caught up in scandals. We witnessed unjust wars, homelessness, drugs and moral degradation. Americans no longer trusted those in authority and even began eyeing their neighbors as enemies. There has been a progressive movement against the government, against religion, against loyalty and honor with employers and family. It has become every man for himself. When people talk about the "American Dream" it's as if it is only an illusion. Unfortunately our nation has never found a solid ideology that could propel us back to greatness.

Americans have become very self serving and indulgent. We've become a nation of takers, not givers. Everyone feels a sense of entitlement, like the government owes him or her. The wealthy won't give up their tax breaks. Ministries won't give up their tax-exempt status. The poor won't give up their welfare, and no one is willing to give up their social security. How can any government survive under those conditions? Americans need to consider what they can offer to help our nation. It's a simple idea. We need to recapture our creative and industrious spirit that once caused us to be dreamers and innovators. People must become resolved to live for more than a work-a-day existence; living from paycheck to paycheck with little or no hope of change. We must stop thriving on appearances with little or no substance. Americans must also become trusting and loyal again. Stop switching employers, divorcing their spouses, moving in and out of homes; from city to city in pursuit of happiness. Being happy is something you choose to be, regardless of your circumstances. Politicians say Americans need jobs! No! Americans need motivation, an impetus to live life with a greater purpose. In our economy, a job is no different from a welfare check. It's slave labor. People are being forced to do whatever is required, just to get paid. No one is being trained to give back into the economic system. Yeah, we talk about saving and investing in America because we value our capitalistic market system, but our greatest resource is our people. We have to be willing to invest in Americans by instilling within them a sense of value in being connected to something bigger than themselves. They need hope of one day contributing to the big picture. This is where the power of God's Kingdom comes in. It's based on the Law of Seedtime and Harvest. You have to sow into the Kingdom, to receive anything from the Kingdom. What you get out of the system, depends upon how much you are willing to give. It is generated from one's heartfelt contribution. The more willing you are to give, the more you will receive.

In God's Kingdom, one's purpose is designed to expand the Kingdom throughout the earth. Therefore, every citizen is required to give back to the Kingdom by ministering to the needs of a particular human concern. It is very common for people to seek God and find out that their purpose includes their gifts, talents, and their passions for life. Also God thinks BIG. People soon realize that their purpose is not about them, but about their family, their city and state as well as their nation and the nations of the world. After all, Jesus commands all those of the Kingdom to *"Go into all the world"* and preach the gospel. This is where many Christians miss it. They don't follow this command because they are comfortable in their American lifestyles. On average, most Christians don't believe in the Kingdom. They believe in the "American Dream." The prosperity movement in the church fed the appetite of materialistic Americans. People were happy to hear that God would give them a nice house or car, but when God told them to sell the house and car and move to Africa to drill wells, they balked. According to the Spirit of God, the world is suffering because American Christians refuse to give up their comfort to help others. America is suffering because Christians refuse to take care of the poor, the widows, the fatherless and strangers as commanded by God. Instead, they send their poor to the government for help. Unfortunately, many Christians panic when things seem scarce, when all they have to do in order to have their needs met, is to obey God and carry out his purpose in their lives.

God has ordained that every human born into this earth has a predetermined mission to fulfill. The "American Dream," is no longer attainable under the Kingdom Age, but when we seek our divine purpose and walk in it, we sow a seed for a greater America. As a result of obeying God in our purpose, we reap a harvest that supersedes a job, training, education, money, home and every satisfaction of this life. We also reap a harvest that changes the world around us for the good. This is true prosperity.

GOD'S KINGDOM ECONOMICS VERSUS THAT OF THE WORLD

There is a myth among some Christian leaders that God does not care about the economies of the world except for that of Israel. They send money to Israel and make sure its people have jobs, but they do nothing for their own neighbors, labeling Americans as sinful, lazy people who God would never waste time prospering. Jesus told us to love our neighbors, especially the poor, widow, homeless and father, and yet pastors shame those in their congregations who are unemployed or homeless, by telling them that if they were really saved and had faith, they would have a job or a home. Many have also been told that if they don't work, they don't eat (II Thessalonians 3:10). Consequently, church leaders have sent their unemployed and poor directly to the county and state offices for assistance. This is one reason America is suffering economically. Politically speaking, these are the same leaders who also complain about too much governmental control. They are the same voices that oppose abortion, because they are pro-life, but their pro-life stance stops once the child is born. They provide neither educational programs nor financial assistance to support the babies they saved from the abortionist. Their solution is to send the people to the state for help.

For America to survive financially, everyone must do his or her part. A great deal of the responsibility is supposed to be on the church, not on the government. While religious leaders complain that the government is too involved, God would say that the church is not involved enough in the affairs of the people he has placed in their care. What has been done is only a drop in the bucket compared to what is needed in this country and around the world. We are the light of the world, yet we have hidden our light under a bushel barrel. This ought not be. Now, some would question. "Does God really care about the economy of America?" Yes! God wants all nations to turn their hearts to him and prosper.

Remember when Daniel was thrown in the lion's den because he refused to bow down to an idol (Daniel Chapter 6)? God shut the lion's mouth and saved Daniel's life. After seeing this miracle (Daniel 6:25-28), King Darius decreed that his entire kingdom bow before the God of Daniel saying, *"for he is the living God, . . . and his dominion shall be even unto the end."* The Bible says that this miracle caused Daniel to prosper during the reigns of Darius and Cyrus the Persian. Daniel, along with God's people were in Babylonian captivity for seventy years, and he prospered. Notice that Daniel prospered because God prospered him in that land. After God shut the lion's mouth it got the attention of an entire nation. Then the nation prospered because they decreed to follow the God of Daniel.

Another great example of a nation being prospered by God was in the days of Joseph. You may recall how Joseph had two dreams from God foretelling of an illustrious future for his life. His brothers were so hateful after hearing about the dreams that they plotted to kill Joseph. Rather than killing him, they threw him in a pit, and told their father that he had been killed by a wild animal. Joseph's brothers were so evil that they took his coat and covered it in animal blood as proof that he was dead. Later they sold Joseph into slavery and eventually he ended up in an Egyptian jail cell (Genesis Chapters 37, 39). It was known in the jail that God gave Joseph the gift of interpreting dreams, and when Pharaoh had a dream and none of his wise men could interpret it, he sent for Joseph (Genesis Chapter 41). Pharaoh's dream was a message from God warning him of a famine that was to come. Not only did God give Joseph the meaning of the dream, but God also gave him a plan of action that saved the world from famine, while making Egypt the wealthiest nation on the earth (Genesis 47:13-26).

Many Christians have been taught that giving and tithing are the keys to God's economic plan for wealth, but an even greater key is at work here: obedience. When we obey (or disobey) God, this is considered sowing a seed in the Kingdom, and for every seed we sow there will be a resulting harvest (whether we expect it or not). Like the Law of Gravity, the Law of Seedtime and Harvest works in the earth regardless of one's knowledge and/or belief in it. Whatever a person has in life is a direct result of the actions they chose to take (Galatians 6:7). If you want a better outcome in life, choose a path that will yield better results. As we discussed earlier in this book, whenever believers obey God, it causes the Blessing to supernaturally provide wealth and prosperity to come upon them and overtake them (Deuteronomy 28:1-14). The Bible promises that Seedtime and Harvest will remain in operation as long as the earth remains (Genesis 8:22). As many ways as there are to obey God, there are just as many ways to obtain wealth and financial success in his Kingdom. The key is finding a seed to sow (to give). Not every seed involves money. It may be a gift or talent shared with another. It could also be anything you have in your possession that could benefit another. In many cases, it will be the Holy Spirit who will lead you to what to sow as seed. God can supernaturally provides for his people who have little or nothing to give. Everyone has seed to sow.

The major difference between God's Kingdom economics and the economies of the world is the idea of *giving to receive*. Again, it is based upon the Law of Seedtime and Harvest. If a farmer wants corn, he has to plant corn seeds in the ground. The same idea is true in God's Kingdom. If you want what God has, you have to sow a seed of obedience to God, to get it. Christians are always "believing God" to bless them. What they are saying is that they are "hoping" God will bless them because they have not completed the steps necessary to receive from God. The process of receiving from God is not complicated. The word of God is called the incorruptible seed of God (I Peter 1:23). Faith begins when the seed of God's word takes root in the hearts of men. By reading and meditating on the word, it will begin to bud within your heart like a seed. All of a sudden there will be a "knowing" in your spirit. This is the Holy Spirit confirming that the promise in the Bible is now available for you. This is the faith that produces Kingdom results in the earth.

Too many Christians don't understand faith and therefore don't see results. They think that if they find a verse in the Bible, they can just ask for it and it should happen for them. No. That is not faith. That is hope. The Bible is filled with seed that will potentially produce a harvest, but that harvest cannot manifest without seed faith; and faith cannot happen without reading and meditating on the word of God. You also have to speak the word. For example, if you want God to save your soul, you have to believe in your heart and confess with your mouth the Lordship of Jesus over life (Romans 10:9). Faith speaks what is in the heart. You will have what you say. The same principal applies if you want healing, or deliverance, or finance or direction. Find the word of God on the subject. Meditate on it in your heart and speak it. That is how you sow.

Some churches spend much time celebrating those who have offerings to give in the collection plate. They seem to forget those who have little or nothing to give can still sow. God makes special arrangements for everyone to get in on a blessing regardless of how much you have to give. II Corinthians 9:10 says that the Lord gives us seed to sow (for a future harvest) and bread for eating. Again, the key to the Blessing is obedience. There was the famine in which the prophet Elijah visited the widow from Zarephath who was about to make her final meal and was preparing to die (I Kings 17:9-16). God sent Elijah to live with the widow. Now, the woman had just enough meal and oil to make a meal for her and her son, but Elijah told her to make a meal for him first (seed), after which the Lord promised that her meal nor oil would run out until the famine ended (harvest). So the woman obeyed. She made a meal cake for Elijah first, and then one for her and her son, and just as the prophet said, her meal and oil remained enough to sustain all three of their lives throughout the famine.

The widow from Zarephath needed food, but there was another widow who needed money. Her husband left her in debt and the creditors were about to seize her sons and take them as slaves (II Kings 4:1-7). The prophet Elisha asked her what she had of value in the house. The woman said that she had only a pot of oil (seed). Elisha told her to go borrow many vessels from her neighbors. When she returned, the prophet had her fill the vessels with the oil from the pot, and as many vessels that she brought, each was filled with oil. When there were no more vessels, the oil stopped flowing. Elisha told the woman to take the vessels and sell the oil to pay her debt. God provided enough money for her to pay the debt and live off the rest with her children (harvest).

Do you have a debt to pay. Maybe a tax bill? Check this out. Apostle Peter was a fisherman by trade and when it came tax time, he had no money to pay the bill. He went to Jesus for help (Matthew 17:24-27). Just like the prophets Elijah and Elisha did in the previous examples, Jesus gave specific instructions to Peter. He told him to cast a fishing hook into the sea and take out the first fish that bites the hook (seed). Jesus told Peter to open the mouth of that fish and there he would find money to pay taxes (harvest). The money was obviously more than Peter needed for himself because Jesus told him to take it to pay taxes for them both. If we do what God says do, we will have what God says we would have.

Now, we will briefly discuss: the tithe, first fruits, and alms giving. The Bible says that the tithe belongs to the Lord (Leviticus 27:30). However, there are some that teach that the tithe is Old Testament and not required under the New Testament (Blood Covenant) of Jesus Christ. The Spirit of God spoke clearly about the importance of the tithe. He said, ***"It may not be required, but it is necessary to fulfill all righteousness."*** Meaning that you won't lose your salvation by not tithing, but you will not fulfill all that is necessary to receive the full benefits of being saved. Under the tithe, there is supernatural protection covering your family and your assets. God also promises to open up his flood gates in Heaven and pour out a blessing that there would not be room enough to receive it (Malachi 3:10-11). We will talk more about tithing in the chapter on taxes. First fruits are different from the tithe. The tithe is a tenth of your income. First fruits are the first of your possessions. It could mean an entire paycheck on a new job. The first proceeds of a business. It is according to your faith, but the benefits are evident. The Bible says to honor the Lord with your possessions and the first fruits of your increase. So that your barns will be filled and your vats overflowing with new wine (Proverbs 3:9-10). In other words, if you want to live in the overflow of God's Kingdom blessings, tithing and fruit fruits are the way to go. Finally, we will touch upon giving to the poor (alms giving). There are some who say there is no benefit in giving to the poor. They believe that it is more beneficial to give people the word instead of meeting their needs. Jesus did not teach this. He fed the people's needs while teaching them principles of Kingdom increase. Even the first apostles had doctrine that required taking care of the poor amongst them (Galatians 2:10). In these last days, God will be transferring wealth to those who will take care of the poor.

This is just an overview of how God's Kingdom provides for the wealth needs of its citizens. This is also how God expects his people to live, especially in times of famine. It is quite different from the US capital market system, but God's Kingdom economics is guaranteed not to fail, no matter who is in political power. The good news is that you don't have to be a Christian to participate in God's system.

Supplemental Reading: To read more personal stories detailing how God is still supernaturally providing for our needs, check out this Ezine Article entitled, *"All We Need is in a Seed"* by Paula Matthews, (http://ezinearticles.com/6707455).

CHAPTER 5

GOD REQUIRES ECONOMIC JUSTICE

THE PURPOSE FOR
THE TRANSFER OF WEALTH

God loves justice (Psalm 37:28). He executes righteousness and judgment for all who are oppressed (Psalm 103:6). Vengeance belongs to God, and he promises to repay us for what we have suffered (Hebrews 10:30). One of the ways God executes judgment is to the transfer money and possessions from the perpetrator of wickedness to those who were oppressed by them. The Bible refers to this as the *recompense of reward* (Hebrews 10:35). There have been several instances in Biblical history where God transferred the wealth of a nation to His People. The most notable was when God brought plagues upon Egypt (Exodus Chapters 7-12) after Pharaoh refused to release God's people who had been enslaved for over four-hundred years. It took ten devastating plagues to convince Egypt that God was all powerful, but it was the final plague that forced the wealth and God's people from the hands of this wicked nation. That plague killed the first born of every Egyptian household except those of the Israelites. Pharaoh called for Moses in the night telling him to get up and go. When God's people left, they plundered Egypt of its wealth. We mention the plagues and the plundering of Egypt because this is exactly the type of experience that will cause the wealth to transfer in America and in the nations of the world. How God will bring it to pass, no one knows for sure. We just take God at his prophetic word and prepare for that day to come.

The questions that should be asked are why is the wealth transfer necessary, and why would God bring the plagues? The easier of the two questions to answer is why transfer the wealth. Before they came to Egypt, the Israelites were pilgrims in search of a promise of someday becoming a nation. The promise was first made to Abraham, but the Lord told him before he could become father of nations, his people would be held captive for over four hundred years. After that time God promised to bring them out with great power and substance. God was so determined to fulfill his promise to Abraham that he allowed Joseph to be enslaved in Egypt, even though Joseph had a dream of great wealth and power. Not only did God give Joseph manifestations of the dream, but he also gave him a plan of action that resulted in Egypt obtaining all the wealth of the world during a time of famine. It was at this time that Joseph stored up wealth that would someday be transferred to the People of God. He became second in command of Egypt and brought his family, and all their people with them to live in Goshen where they became a mighty people both in numbers and in substance. There are several key points that we need to highlight. First, Joseph was born into a family of privilege but was made a slave. It was the covenant promise of God that would restore him to his divine position with great wealth and power. Many years after Joseph, another Pharaoh enslaves the people because their great numbers intimidated him. They were enslaved for four hundred thirty years. Their generations were born and raised as Egyptians, far removed from the Abrahamic covenant. When they cried out in their captivity, it was Almighty God that remembered his covenant and sent Moses to deliver his people. Here is a mystery of God's Kingdom that continues to repeat throughout history. Great wealth and power in God's Kingdom is gained by suffering through obedience. The rewards are not always promised to occur on this side of Heaven, but the rewards and honor will always come.

The Children of Israel realized that *The Lord is a man of war* (Exodus 15:3) who would show his strength on behalf of those who trust in him. Our trust is demonstrated when we obey God no matter how uncomfortable things get. God calls us to be warriors for the Kingdom. A warrior is valiant; one who boldly stands for the honor of his King and Kingdom, even until death. When we stand obediently against oppression, human degradation, worldwide injustice, God honors us. This does not mean that we blindly take up a cause. It means that each of us is called to a specific task that will require obedience in the midst of persecution, death threats and dishonor of men. If God has ordained it for us, we must stand order to accomplish a Kingdom mandate. It is when the mission is completed that God gives the reward. Most warriors don't look for battles to fight, they are called by the circumstances that arise. There was One however, who knew his task and what was required of him, long before the foundation of the world. Perhaps the greatest warrior story ever told was that of Jesus Christ, who knowingly gave up his heavenly honor and wealth to deliver us from oppression of the devil. Then he gave up his earthly life so that we could have the abundant life that God originally designed for us. Isaiah prophesied about the rewards Jesus would gain because of his suffering on earth for all humanity (Isaiah 53). He tells how men despised Jesus and brutally killed him. Men also thought that Jesus was rejected by God, but he was not. It pleased God to afflict his son. Hebrews 12:2 says that for the joy of seeing us gain the promise of God, Jesus endured the cross and its shame. When Jesus hung on the cross he said, *"It is finished"* when he knew that the will of God for his life had been accomplished. It was then that he died (John 19:28-30), and today he is still reaping the rewards of his mission. Isaiah said that when God saw the suffering and travail of his soul, he rewarded him great spoils because he poured out his life unto death, which would result in the souls of men being reconciled back to God. Notice that the prophet said men would be reconciled back to God. This lets us know that mankind would be restored to God's original position and plan for their lives. What was this position and plan? Look at Adam and Eve. The position was that of sons and daughters of God. The plan was for them to be caretakers and heirs of this earth (Genesis 2:15). Adam sinned and lost this earth. Jesus came to restore everything that Adam lost. He restored the Blessing and released mankind from the curse. This is the grace of God towards all men. Our reconciliation was complete in Christ. God was not going to be satisfied until everything was restored back to us. We were delivered from the power of darkness and translated into the Kingdom (Colossians 1:13). We were restored as sons of God (John 1:12); heirs of God and joint heirs with Jesus (Romans 8:16-17). We who have received the abundance of grace and the gift of righteousness shall reign in life by the One Jesus Christ (Romans 5:17). In this restoration, we were made kings and priest unto our God (Revelation 5:10), the royals sons of God, and heirs of this world.

Here is where suffering comes into play for the believer. We are to continue what Jesus did in this earth; opening the eyes of the world to turn them from darkness to light; from the power of Satan back to God; so that they may receive forgiveness of sins and receive their inheritance (Acts 26:18). Jesus is sending us into darkness to rescue the lost, but Satan always opposes us. Nevertheless, we must obey God, if we want the reward. Suffering in obedience to God carries with it great rewards in the Kingdom, but people don't like to suffer. We are all about comfort. Suffering is an idea that most Western minds cannot comprehend, but it is key to the wisdom and riches of God's Kingdom. His ways and thoughts are far beyond human wisdom (Isaiah 55:8-9). That is why it is unwise to live a Christian life in our human understanding. We need the Holy Spirit to guide us to the perfect will of the Father.

God has spoken through his prophets saying that *he was raising up a remnant in America who will obey him*. These are the ones who will receive all the wealth similar to what happen with the Children of Israel during the days of Moses. Decades ago there were many prophecies coming forth in Los Angeles about God raising up powerful Black men and women in His next great move across the nation. I recall one White pastor who heard the prophecy and jokingly said that he was going to have to find a way to marry into a Black family just to get in on what God was doing. A few years after that, the Lord began pointing out Barack Obama as the next president. This was confirmation to the Body of Christ that this highly anticipated move of God had begun. Then in 2011, when the turmoil began in Egypt and North Africa, the Holy Spirit said that *the move of God was sweeping over all who were of African Blood*. Black, White, or Arab didn't matter any more. God was showing up and speaking to those of African blood. Jesus Christ was appearing in dreams and visions and Arab and African people are converting to Christianity in record numbers. That is why there have been so many killings in the Middle East and Africa. This wave of the Spirit is about to hit America as well. When it does, many valiant warriors will take center stage, and like their African brothers, be willing give up their lives for the cause of Christ. Not all will die in the fight, but we all must die to our own selfish desires. This is required of all Kingdom warriors. It is then that God can restore, wealth, honor and position to whom it is due.

The restoration of honor back to God is the greatest reason for the wealth transfer. In the case of the captives in Egypt, they had been working the land for over four hundred years without maintaining the sacrificial worship to God. Whenever a people are in covenant with God, he will get the honor and worship due his name, even if it means overturning a powerful nation and making them pay from their own pockets. This is what happened in Egypt. God wanted the captives released, and Egypt refused to honor God after Joseph had helped the nation become very prosperous. They boasted in their wealth and gave honor to their numerous gods rather than to the Almighty God who had used Joseph to solidify their wealthy place in the world. God told Pharaoh to release his first born (Israel), or God would kill their first born. This was strong covenant talk coming from God. Ultimately it was the death of the first born in Egypt that forced Pharaoh to release the People of God. The wealth was freely given to the captives as an appeasement to God, and in the wilderness a proper sacrifice was made by the Israelites to the

God of Abraham. Similarly, America has been greatly blessed by God, but we have not given him the honor due his name. Like Egypt, our nation has forgotten that it was God who gave us the power to get wealth (Deuteronomy 8:18). Instead we pay homage to the many gods of our capitalistic markets as the source of our power and wealth. The people are being oppressed and are crying out to God. He is about to send deliverers to release the people from their captors and transfer all the wealth in the process. According to the Spirit of God, ***"The people have been cheated and defrauded of all their labors in the American system. They pay more and yet receive so little benefit from their labors as their wealthy lords of business, industry and government live off the fat of the land at the expense of those they oppress. No more says God. Not in this land. Not in My America!"***

WEALTH TRANSFER MEANS A REGIME CHANGE!

When the Spirit of God began speaking to me about this section he said that the wealth transfer would mean *"A regime change"* in America. Now, this does not mean a natural change as much as it does a spiritual change. God's Kingdom is about to rule in America. No longer will business or government be able to function as it has in past decades. The supernatural plan of God has even now been revealed to select individuals who are about to be sent out to help the government and the nation to prosper. These are not politically oriented people. They are God's Kingdom ambassadors sent to America as their duty to God. These brave men and women will step out with God's plan for different industries and wealth development, entertainment and inventions; things that the government can't do, and the church has long refused to do. These valiant warriors will produce what God wants in the earth and the wealth will flow, and the people will rejoice.

The regime change has to begin in the Christian church in America, where pastors and leaders are used to doing their own thing regardless of what God desires. It's been a long process, but God finally has a remnant of people who will listen and obey his commands. They will go into industry and produce Kingdom results that will benefit all men regardless of their race or religion. The issue with the church has been the mindset of Christians who believe that God only cares about what happens in the church building. Christianity is not a religion. It is a way of living in the earth that produces the Blessing instead of the curse. The

Kingdom of God is bigger than the church. It's purpose is to overthrow all other Kingdoms (Daniel 2:44) so that the Blessing can overtake the curse of poverty, famine, disease and suffering that is in the earth today. So often the church itself is suffering because they just don't understand how the power of Jesus' death and resurrection can transform their lives and the world around them.

The church is also suffering because they did not obey God's command to *go into all the world* (Mark 16:15). Many thought it meant going as a missionary to foreign countries, and they shut God down because they didn't want to go. The first mission for every believer is their own household; their neighbors and others they meet on a daily basis (Acts 1:8). While preachers will deliver a message from a pulpit in a church, individual Christian lives are the messages that people observe. Again, we are ambassadors of God's Kingdom. When people observe that we are living in wealth, health and prosperity while others are suffering, they will ask what we are doing differently. If you lost your job in a particular industry and a former coworker saw you thriving without a job. They would automatically ask what you are doing differently? These are God ordained opportunities to tell them about how the Kingdom operates. Unfortunately because so many Christians are bellyaching about their losses and complaining about what the government should do for them, people don't desire to come to the Kingdom. How can they come unless someone shows them the way? How can Christians show the way unless they decide to obey God to obtain Kingdom results for themselves? Only through obedience will Christians lives draw others into the Kingdom of God.

When Jesus commanded us to *"Go"* some people shared their vision from God about building schools and businesses and even about creating inventions. God had given them an area to target their gifts and talents, but it was those trusted mentors and confidants in the church who told them that their vision was not from God. Ignorantly, people gave up the vision of God and became ministers and pastors in the church. The pervasive mindset of the church is that God only calls people into the traditional ministry of the church. Not so! The word ministry is misunderstood because we automatically think of religion and church work, but this word describes a service done by a minister (servant) to the public. This term is also used in nations around the world to describe departments within a country's government structure. Countries that use these titles most often have Prime Ministers as well. God's Kingdom has ministries of missions, outreach and businesses around the world. Each serves a specific public need. God doesn't necessarily want us to abandon our professions, but rather use our professions for the benefit of the Kingdom. In America, if someone is called into ministry, we immediately think it means preaching in a pulpit and working full-time in a church, but that is not always the case. This is often the reason people hesitate about answering the call of God for their lives.

God is the Creator of this earth. He is ultimately concerned about people and their living conditions in the earth. The Christian message is about setting human beings free from poverty, sickness, disease, bondage, and lack, and restoring to them the abundant life that God provided in the Garden of Eden. Given this, God's Kingdom has Ministers of Defense against demonic and human bondage, Ministers of Health and Healing; Ministers of Public Finance, Public Education, etc. Each person entering into the Kingdom of God is automatically assigned to one or more departments of ministry. It is up to each person to find out where they have been assigned and to complete their assignments as is pleasing to God.

Expect a resurgence of entrepreneurs in America. There will be people coming forth with schools and teaching methods especially designed with solutions that current schools have never considered. There will be self-sustaining businesses that recognize the importance of excellence in product quality and customer service above making money. Real creativity will begin to flow again because the Creator is releasing a fresh look and sound that will be seen and heard throughout the media.

Entertainment and media will offer a variety of triumphant success oriented stories that will uplift and motivate their viewers. There will be an emergence of business economic models that look vastly different from what we see today because the purpose is divinely motivated. The current leading economic indicators will be obsolete. A spiritual wave of innovation is coming that will challenge everything we have been taught about doing business on earth. God is about to confound all of human wisdom. America will be God's Kingdom test model. The world will see us prosper and desire to know our secret. The secret things belong to God (Deuteronomy 29:29), and he is about to reveal them to his people as their inheritance, to benefit all mankind.

WHAT SHALL BE GIVEN TO HIM WHO SLAYS THIS GIANT?

"Choose a Man to Come Down to Me. If He is Able to Fight and Kill Me Then We Will be Your Servants."(Goliath) I Samuel 17:8-9

The word of the Lord came to me in the form of a political commentary. The Spirit of the Lord said, ***"The current (Obama) administration has inherited a Goliath (economic) that no previous administration has ever wanted to slay. God is sending his "Davids" onto the field for the purpose of taking this giant's head."*** The Lord let me hear the ugly political comments and remarks about the President's handling of economic issues. He then showed me that the comments were being hurled at the President because no one else has any idea of how to help our country. No one is offering any solutions, only criticism. It was then that the Lord reminded me of what happened when David offered to kill Goliath. He was sorely criticized. The giant was terrorizing the armies and the people. No one was willing to go onto the field to fight, and yet they were quick to criticize David for his boldness to step forward. In America, our Goliath is the economy, and God is about to send help to this administration, they are our Davids in this hour.

In David's time, just like ours, we are transitioning from a nation where the people's choice rules, to a nation whose leaders are being led by the Spirit of God. And just like David, these leaders may not necessarily be trained for the task that they will undertake, but they will be able to slay giants without Saul's armor. They will not need conventional military armor or weapons because this is a spiritual battle that can only be won by the supernatural. I will warn you not to be so hasty in bad mouthing the ideas or methods that God's leaders may use to take down the giant. God is about to use the foolish things of this world to compound the wisdom of those who think they know it all. David was able to bypass military protocol to slay Goliath with one smooth stone and a slingshot, and so it will be with the new leaders who are about to take center stage.

GOD (NOT POLITICIANS) GIVES US POWER TO GET WEALTH

"How long will you remain simple-minded? How long will you relish in mocking and fools hate knowledge?" Proverbs 1:22

I heard the voice of Wisdom crying in the streets of the nation and around the world. She was crying out to those who had heard the instruction of the Lord concerning beginning businesses, banking and educational institutions and other venues of economic development. Most people have refused to implement the plan that God gave them. Many questioned in their hearts why it was necessary to start new organizations when others were struggling. Did it ever occur to them that God had a different way of conducting business? Did it ever enter into their minds that God had inside information that something was about to happen. What about needing to build an **"ark of protection"** for our families, community and the nation?

I was reminded of all the ministers and leaders who bragged about what God told them to do. A few of them obeyed what they heard. Because America has been so prosperous, Christians just assume that our nation's prosperity would last forever. NO! It was God who gave us the power to get wealth, but it came with a warning. In Deuteronomy 8:18-19, God said that if we forget him and claim that our wealth was by our own strength, he would cause us to perish. Virtually, no public figure in America gives glory to God for what he has given us, and yet for the sake of the faithful believers in this land, God will not forsake us.

Heed the voice of the Lord today! *God gives his greatest treasures for financial success during times of famine.* One word of instruction from God can transform your entire financial future. It will also give the American economy her greatest boost. Great rewards await those who will heed the voice of God and prepare the business or institution. God has promised to transfer immense wealth to those who obey him in this economic mission. God will do it to prove that his Kingdom financial incentives are better than anything the US Government could ever offer. With God's spiritual and financial backing, Kingdom enterprises will thrive in any and all market conditions.

ARE YOU POSITIONED TO RECEIVE WEALTH?
"The Wealth of the Wicked is Laid up for the Just" Proverbs 13:22
The Lord has just declared that, **"The Wealth Transfer is Here!"** God reminded me that most of the Body of Christ is expecting wealth, but not all are qualified. The Lord quoted Proverbs 13:22 and said that he wanted to clarify who is *wicked* (sinner) and who is *just*. God requires that *the just shall live by their faith*. So, although Christians are looking for wealth, only those who are obedient will actually get it. In fact, there are even wicked people in the church who will loose the wealth that they now possess, if they don't change. God said that as long as they con-

tinue their wickedness, he will refuse to let certain of his people have wealth. To do otherwise would be perceived as God's endorsement of hypocrisy and sin among his people.

Why should God give you wealth to spend upon your evil lusts? He won't do it. If you want the wealth, you have to be prepared to receive it. That requires heeding the voice of God concerning the specific mission for that money. When the Children of Israel left slavery and plundered the wealth of Egypt, it was so that they could worship God with it. God gives us the power to get wealth to establish his covenant with us. The wealth is scheduled to come to those who are covenant minded. In addition, the Lord brought to my attention that it was not only God's covenanted people who got the wealth, but there was also a mixed multitude (Exodus 12:38) of those who were not of the seed of Abraham, but who chose to follow the God of Abraham.

Likewise, God will also transfer wealth into the Kingdom by converting the souls of many who are already wealthy. Like Zacchaeus who was a wealthy tax collector, he received Jesus and offered to give half of his possessions to the poor, and he offered to pay back four times the amount that he had stolen from others (Luke 19:1-10). Those who will hear and obey God will get the wealth.

If you want to position yourselves for wealth, repent and turn from your sin. Then inquire of God what he would have you do for His Kingdom. Write the vision and make it plain (Habakkuk 2:2), so when the money comes, you can run with it! Let him who has an ear to hear receive what the Lord is saying to the church.

CHAPTER 6

GOD ORDERS EQUAL TAXATION

"Doth not your master pay tribute?"
Matthew 17:24

When it comes to the question of Christians paying taxes it should suffice just to say *"Render to Caesar that which is Caesars; and unto God that which is God's* (Luke 20:25),*"* but the Holy Spirit revealed why it is necessary for believers to pay taxes. In Jesus' day, they paid tribute for temple tax in addition to paying what was required by the civil authorities of his day. When collectors came to Peter for temple tax (Matthew 17:24-27), they asked if Jesus was in the habit of paying as well. Why would they ask Peter about whether Jesus paid taxes? Why didn't they just ask Jesus directly? Jesus answers this question by asking Peter a question. Jesus asked Peter, *"From whom do kings of the earth collect taxes; of their own children or of strangers?"* Peter answered, *"Of strangers"* and Jesus agreed by saying, *"Then are the children free from paying."* Jesus had this conversation concerning taxes right after Peter, James and John witnessed his being transfigured on the mountain and Elijah and Moses appeared to him (Matthew 17:1-13). They also heard the voice of God speak from Heaven saying, *"This is my beloved Son in whom I am well pleased; hear ye him."*

So, why did Jesus ask Peter about how earthly taxes were collected? They were being asked to pay taxes for the temple (House of God) and by right Jesus who is the Son of God should not be entitled to pay taxes for his Father's house. Jesus was saying that even though he was not entitled to pay, he chose to pay taxes so that the authorities would not be offended (Matthew 17:27).

In America we are in the habit of avoiding taxes, but in the eyes of God, we should always pay taxes to whom it is due. It has everything to do with honoring those to whom honor is due. Apostle Paul explains it so well in Romans 13:1-7. He explains that we are to submit ourselves to the governing authorities because they are ordained by God. To rebel against authority is to rebel against what God established. Paul urged God's people to do what was right so that they could obtain honor from the authorities. He also said we should pay taxes so that the government can pay its debts. God also has a tax to run his Kingdom. It is called the tithe. The tithe is requested from everyone in God's Kingdom to make sure there is enough to pay God's bills. When believers don't pay tithes (one tenth of our income) they are robbing God of the honor he so greatly deserves (Malachi 3:8-12). Psalm 24:1 says that the earth and all that it has belongs to the Lord. We should be delighted to honor God for giving us life and liberty in the earth, and yet so many Christians refuse to tithe. Similarly, paying taxes is our way of honoring the authorities for having allowed us the use of their land and utilities for our business, ministry and livelihood. Again, just like the tithe, so many American's do whatever they can to get out of paying taxes. There are Christian ministries that thrive on their IRS tax-exempt status, and yet they complain because this status requires that they cannot endorse a specific political candidate. The one common thing about both tithes and taxes, not paying them is an indicator of how one feels about that authority. Jesus said, where your treasure is, so will your heart be also (Luke 12:34). This is very true. When people try to find ways to avoid giving honor where it is due, it means that they don't really honor that authority, otherwise they would freely give.

Here is a direct quote given to me by the Holy Spirit concerning the taxation in America: ***"God is about to overthrow the church, but a remnant will arise and obey. There will be two worlds one of which will be obedient to God that will prosper because God will transfer all the wealth to them. They will run God's Kingdom on earth as it is in Heaven. Oh! They won't care about tax breaks or tax loopholes. They will render to Caesar that which is rightfully Caesar's and undergird the financial health of America. Some would argue that the tax breaks are legal; I'd say, 'So Is Abortion!' Both are against God's Kingdom operation; so even to obey such in America means to be in the curse and not the Blessing. Remember Joseph in Egypt's famine? God gave him a tax plan that was designed to bring wealth to the country. This is where America missed it! Without taxes; The Country Cannot Survive!"***

CHAPTER 7

GOD'S KINGDOM AGE HAS BEGUN!

THE KINGDOM OF GOD IS ARISING IN OUR MIDST
"God's Kingdom shall break into pieces and consume all other kingdoms; and His Kingdom shall stand forever." Daniel 2:44

God's Kingdom is advancing with supernatural power across the earth. The Lord's mighty army is ferociously taking on the enemy in the War on Oppression. It's a fierce battle that began in Heaven and will resolve on the earth, as God sets the captives free; free from human slavery, free from economic oppression and human degradation. It's a spiritual battle to expose and destroy the forces of darkness that have kept people bound to poverty, abuse and lack.

Politicians can blame it on the opposition party, but what plagues America is systemic. It's a generational curse of men creating and sustaining wealth at the expense of others; a win-lose operation that perpetuates wealth for the wealthy and poverty for the poor. So, whose fault is it? The Spirit of God blames the American Church. Many American church leaders are praying against our country in hopes that she will fail, and in the meantime the people are being oppressed as they fear for their livelihood.

God hates oppression and has declared by His Spirit that, *"The oppressors must be subdued."* His first battle is to subdue the oppressors in the church. God is about to unveil his plan in America. There is coming a separation between those who profess religion versus those who follow Jesus Christ, the obedient ones who imitate the love and compassion of their father.

THE FIERCE WINDS OF CHANGE ARE
BLOWING IN OUR DIRECTION
"And suddenly there came a sound from heaven like a rushing mighty wind . . ." Acts 2:2

America is about to experience a major transformation that has been initiated by Almighty God. There is a shift occurring in the spirit that is repositioning leadership and ideology in a manner unlike anything we have seen in history. There is a divine reordering happening in our midst; a transformation that no human or political faction can deter. The Spirit of God is about to confound the wise and confuse the simple. The only ones who will emerge with understanding and wisdom will be the true Believers of Jesus Christ; those who truly know God. In this hour, do not judge anything by its appearance alone. Deception will be rampant among us. Nothing will be as it seems. Nothing will be as it was. Problems won't be resolved like before. We have come to the end of ourselves and the only possible way out is through God. This is message is for the church. This message is for politicians. This message is for business owners and executives and the common man on the street. Change is here.

Dear Christian, this is your final examination before Jesus returns. You will be tested on your learning and comprehension of his Word. You will be tested on recognizing his voice over all other voices. Your faith will be sorely tested. Are you ready to be put to the test?

So what can one do to prepare? Make peace with God and seek his direction about every decision you make. This is critical. Human wisdom will fail in this hour. Ungodly wisdom will fail. Listen to God. Obey God, and watch him move miraculously in your house, your business, your city, and our nation.

No matter how bad it looks, America will arise out of the ashes victoriously and it will astound the world!

CHAPTER 8

NEW LEADERSHIP FOR A NEW AGE

WHAT DOES GOD THINK ABOUT AMERICAN POLITICS?
"The Heart of the King is in the Hand of the Lord" Proverbs 21:1
Did you know that all throughout the Bible, God chose leaders of nations? It matters to God which leader is ruling over his people. Christians are commanded to submit to those who are in authority, therefore God would never choose an evil person to rule over our nation. When God's people choose leaders whom God has chosen, the nation will prosper, but unfortunately most Christians refuse to vote according to what God is saying. Consequently, God does not blame politicians for the failures in America. He blames the Church. If Christians would obey God, not only in their everyday lives, but also in their ballot choices, then the Hand of God would direct the actions of our leaders. Even if our candidate does not win, we still have an obligation to pray for that person who is over us. Then God can direct that leader's path.

Here's the prophetic view the American political system.
"The American political system is corrupt and full of adulterous men and women. These elected officials have only one true loyalty, and that is to doing whatever it takes to get elected. There is an absence of bold leadership and integrity in American politics and industry. We have groomed many 'yes men' and 'that a boys' who do what they are told. We are experiencing the fallout of this conspiracy of corruption that has resulted in the current financial downfall of our major corporations nation-wide. The average American has had to forfeit their dreams because our political and business leaders have devised wicked plans that promote their own political and financial profit at the expense of all others." Excerpt from "Conclusion," The Conclusion of the Whole Matter, *The War Journal (1999-2010) Volume* I by Paula Matthews.

THE SONS OF GOD ARISING IN THE EARTH!
One of my team members was awaken at 2 am by the Spirit of God. She said that he took her to the Book of Romans and began speaking about things that were happening in the earth. What really set her flying was Romans 8:14. She began exclaiming to our entire group, "this

is who we are! We are the Sons of God!" It dawned on her that each of us was pulled out of our industries and given a vision by God for that particular industry, and because we are obeying the voice of God, that makes us the Sons of God. In all her excitement I reminded her of the vision God gave me in 1998 about the Sons of God he was bringing forth in the earth. Then, the Lord showed this mighty army of leaders by continent. He showed me Eurasia and the seventy-five men and women there. Then there were about seventy-five in all of the Americas and the Caribbean. Finally the Lord showed me the largest number of his Sons in Africa and the Middle East. Unfortunately, these are the same Sons who are willingly giving up their lives in the battle.

God's mighty army is arising in the earth! These are the Sons of God armed with the vision of God for the world. We may fall, but we will not fail in our mission to bless the world, subdue the oppressors of the world, and replenish the earth with the resources God's people so dearly need. This is our mission. Although impossible for mere men, we know that with God, all things are possible!

"In 1998, the Lord took me by the spirit and showed me a small powerful congregation of no more than 200-300 men and women, all of whom had worldwide ministries. The Lord declared this to be His Church that He was raising up in our midst. When I saw these leaders, I was awestruck. They were mighty men and women of valor. Not only did they possess tremendous financial wealth, but superior spiritual strength. All of the ministry gifts and all of the gifts of the Spirit operated through each individual as the Lord willed. They did not seem to be human. They were so much like supernatural beings, that I asked the Lord if they were angels. He told me these were the believers who lived only by His Word and obeyed His Spirit. The Lord said that they would do whatever He asked them to do, without considering themselves or their situations. They were pure and yielded vessels. Each of them performed the greater works Jesus spoke about in John 14:12. They also walked in an unusual power of God that surpassed the works of Moses, Elijah, Elisha, Jesus, and all the Apostles combined." Excerpts from *The War Journal (1999-2010) Volume I* by Paula Matthews.

THE CROWN OF LIFE: OUR INCREASE FOR ENDURING THE BATTLE

"Blessed is the Man Who Endures Temptation; For After He is Tried He Shall Receive the Crown of Life" James 1:12

The Spirit of God declared **2012: The Year of Increase**, but what is required to obtain that increase from God? To find the answer to this question, the Lord called me into a period of fasting and prayer. In a vision, the Spirit of God showed me a time line of human existence that began at creation and extended into eternity.

He showed how he carefully selected specific time frames and specific people and events within each time frame to accomplish his mission to reclaim the earth as His Earthly Kingdom. Theologically speaking, we would call these time frames *special dispensations* of God's Spirit. Then the Lord showed how he specifically chose to use the Body of Christ as a spiritual ***"Trojan horse"*** to infiltrate and overtake evil territories and end the satanic war of world oppression, so that he (God) might bestow upon his mighty faithful warriors the highest military honors ever awarded by the Kingdom of God upon men. There will never be another time like the time in which we live. There will never be another people chosen and equipped to excel in battle over the evil that has gripped the hearts and souls of men for thousands of years, and for those who faithfully accomplish their kingdom orders; they shall receive the Crown of Life. This is our INCREASE for going into combat and enduring the battle.

Just like the Old Testament heroes and Early Church Apostles, future generations in the next millennium and beyond will read about our stories. We are the Last Apostles. There are none after us; neither will there be another age like the one in which we live. We are the warriors called to battle and win for the Kingdom. We are called and equipped for the ultimate victory against all the evil of this generation. ***"And those who dare to believe will arise; and yes there will be many who will arise and stand boldly against the evil of this age and cripple the powers of darkness; yeah even crush Satan under our feet."*** We are victors ready to run to the battle and reclaim territory and release the captives from their evil oppressors in order to resume the plan of peace and prosperity God designed for the earth.

This is God's grand design for mankind, not as man designed, but a plan of equity for all men regardless of their wealth or position. Every need will be supplied and every desire fulfilled when God's Kingdom is fully realized in the millennium. *"And such peace; glorious peace will reign in the earth. Such as never was seen except at creation." "This is my plan," says God; "To increase you more and more you and your children; that you might acquire the inheritance that I have planned for your welfare since the beginning of the world. Yeah it is an earthly inheritance more than you can imagine. . . . And it is yours for the taking for all who would believe."*

CONCLUSION

AMERICAN VALUES REDEFINED
"For where your treasure is, so will your heart be also."
Matthew 6:21

America's treasure used to be God, family and country. Families used to share precious moments around the dinner table. We use to laugh more. We use to take time to smell the roses along our way to work. Americans use to honor those in authority by saying, "yes ma'am" and "yes sir." There was a time where you could seal a contract with a man's word and a handshake, but not any more. Americans have become arrogant, self-centered and cynical. We are no longer our brother's keeper nor do we love our neighbors. What happened to us? We took God out of our lives. Once upon a time our hearts were with God, and he was able to bless and prosper us, but the past fifty-plus years have seen a conscience effort by Americans to separate from God. Rather than making laws that are consistent with the Biblical view, America has compromised its liberty so far as to treat God and Christianity with disdain.

The idea of discussing gay marriage or abortion in the public square would have been considered obscene in years past. These issues have always been considered a private matter of discussion among families and the clergy. Here we are in a new millennium and we are legislating morality so that people with differing lifestyles can live together without violating the right to their own pursuit of happiness. This ought not be!

Even with these highly debated topics bombarding our media, there is a deeper concern that Americans no longer value truth. Far too many Americans don't even believe that truth exists. They think that everyone has a different truth, so how can there be absolute truth? We tend to take things at face value because to do otherwise may make us appear to be judgmental or heretical. But without the pursuit of truth, we cannot have the Blessing God desires for us. Sure, we have achieved great wealth and power, but at the expense of moral degradation and oppression of the poor and weak among us. This is why we are now suffering economically. When we took God out of our lives, we also removed love. God is love, and those who love, are of God (I John 4:8). Unfortunately you can't love God if you don't love yourself. If you are saved, then God is in you. We love him because he first loved us and gave his son for us. We should love what he has done in, and for us. If you don't love yourself, you cannot love your neighbor. After all, to love one's neighbor means that we would not inflict pain or hardship upon them.

Americans value fame and popularity because it is a way to achieve goodness in the eyes of the public without actually being good. It's an illusion that keeps love out, and causes us to distance ourselves from others. This can be seen with the explosive interest in reality TV. We want to be voyeurs in the lives of the rich and famous. We entertain ourselves by enjoying the perversity and dysfunction of others. Americans value degradation of all that seems good and honorable in the world. Our cynicism would cause one to view an innocent action of philanthropy or good will with suspicion because we don't believe that good things happen any more. We don't believe that people desire to be good. This is such a far cry from how things used to be fifty years ago. Back then, we loved and trusted more because we believed in God's Blessing and his ability to make things right for those who had faith. So what happened that we no longer believe? Our idols fell from grace in the eyes of the public. Truth is, men by nature were created to worship God, but when we worship money, people, possessions, or professional accolades instead, this is considered idolatry. We worship people and things because they temporarily fulfill our emotional and psychological needs. But the thing about idols is that they always fail our expectations. An idol can never give to us what a Holy God can. An idol may give you money, but it cannot guarantee you wealth. An idol may give you professional esteem, but it won't keep you from moral or ethical decline. Look at the people we have idolized; movie stars, musicians, celebrities who may have money and fame, but they know it is not real, nor will it last forever. Many whom we idolize are tormented by demons of failure and self-hatred on the inside. They know the truth, but somewhere in their minds they think that if they ignore the obvious, that the person on the inside will one day be what people think he or she really is.

Before America can turn back to God, the American Christian Church must turn from its rebellion against God. Christians are supposed to be like a city set upon a hill (Matthew 5:14), a beacon of life in a dying world. Our illuminated good works draw men to God, but our religious debates in the political arena only serve to make people turn even further away from God. The church has made the mistake of trying to scare people into obeying God. It does not work. The Gospel of the Kingdom is good news. Jesus said that if we would preach the Kingdom like he did, he would cause signs and wonders to confirm the word. So, what did Jesus do? He came preaching the word to set the captives the free, and as they got free, they were healed and delivered; whatever they lacked was restored to them. Now, that's good news, but how many preachers are preaching it? Not many. There is a religious view in America that no matter what Jesus says, people won't come to God unless they are made aware of sin, hell and death. No! No! No! We need to turn from doing and saying our own thing on God's holy day (Isaiah 58:13). We should be preaching what Jesus preached.

Jesus didn't teach sin, hell and death. He taught life, the abundant life in God's Kingdom. That's why he came. He restored to the earth, the Blessing that Adam lost. So all who believe in Jesus (those who obey him) would prosper in this life, and be with him for an eternity. Prospering means more than gaining wealth. It is about living the highest level of human life that God designed for us at creation. It means succeeding at everything God has given us to perform in this life. The God kind of life is the Blessing personified. It means living in the overflow of God's goodness; abounding in every area of life, and whatever is lacking, God will supply from his vast treasury in Heaven.

Remember that the Kingdom of God is *"solution oriented."* God will give wealth to those who desire do with it as He wills. The wealth God gives is to establish his covenant, not to supply the human lust for the finer things in life. God will give wealth to promote and establish the missions he has ordained for the people of the earth. Take the issue of abortion. The church is adamant about fighting abortion, and so they should be, because God hates abortion. Here is the problem. They don't educate their congregations about why God hates abortion. There are so few programs that counsel and monitor Christians who are actively seeking abortions. Instead of fighting with groups like Planned Parenthood, the church should have alternative agencies that teach prevention from God's Kingdom perspective. Sex education is not being taught in the church, it is being left up to public schools who are teaching the world's view, which is opposite to God's views. It is wrong to attempt to force the world to obey God, when the church refuses to obey him.

There are hurting people who have had abortions sitting in congregations around the nation. These people are filled with shame about having had an abortion, but they can't share their hearts because the church is too judgmental. There are others who refuse to come to God because the church has condemned them for having abortions. God will make the church pay for the sufferings they have ignored. Equally appalling is the idea that the church will fight against abortion because they value the sanctity of life, yet they have not developed adequate faith based programs to help these mothers take care of themselves and their babies.

These people are in desperate need of loving care and education on how to be a parent, but where is the church? How can you value an unborn child you don't see, and yet despise those that you do see? This is not the love of God. This is hypocrisy. It's obvious that the world is not able to comprehend the things of the spirit, but unfortunately, the Church can't see either because of the plank in its eye. They act like those in this world who don't have eyes to see, nor ears to hear, or a heart that can perceive the things of God. The Apostle Paul said that the natural man is not subject to God, nor can he be (I Corinthians 2:14). The Church has been reacting, but not taking dominion as God would have them respond to this crisis in our day. There is a need for strong spiritual discernment.

Sinners sin because they don't God. That is why the Bible says that unless a man is born again, he is not able to perceive the things of God's Kingdom (John 3:3), so beating the world over the head with the Bible will not help them see things God's way. There are Christians who read the Bible and they still don't understand the ways of God. The only way the world can begin to see and hear is if they are born again. No one can come to God unless the Holy Spirit draws them (John 6:44), but here is good news. If Christians would do their part and pray for all men (I Timothy 2:1), then the Spirit of God would be free to move in the lives of those around us. Christians are to be the light, but the Holy Spirit is the one who convicts (John 16:8) the world of sin (not us). They must first walk in love and forgive those in the world who are ignorant of spiritual matters.

Whether Christian or not, many Americans are adulterers and idolaters. They would rather do their own thing than obey the rules of those who are in authority, whether it is business, government or religious leaders. We are a stiff-necked people. We are some of the wealthiest people in the world, but we have valued the creation above the Creator. God is about to let us come to the end of ourselves. The U.S. economy does not need more businesses or jobs, or tax breaks to flourish. We need a spiritual awakening. Conditions in the world will continue to deteriorate, and God will let us fall until we return to him. God will return the Blessing to this nation when we learn to honor what he honors. God will return to us when we turn away from our adulterous hearts and begin to worship him again. When we do, God will open the heavens and give us blessings that are far beyond human expectation. When we value what God values (his love and his truth), and pursue him diligently, he will cause the Blessing to come upon us and overtake us. God will withhold no good thing from those who love him. You might not achieve fame in this life, but you will be among the celebrated sons of God who will reign in this life and spend an eternity in a heavenly paradise with our Father God.

For America to survive the economic destruction of the world order, it has no choice but to value what God values. We must think about our neighbor more than ourselves. We need to give freely of our time, talent and finances to honor a cause greater than ourselves. **We must do unto others as we would want them to do unto us.** It's time out for hoarding wealth and building bigger barns for ourselves. This is the prophetic season of Seedtime and Harvest. What you give will come back to you in good measure, pressed down and shaken together and running over will men give back to you (Luke 6:38). This will work for the individual, for a family, a community, a nation and keep working until the entire world is blessed.

QUESTIONS AND ANSWERS
(The Author provides the following questions and answers for your enrichment.)

So, what will our future look like in America? According to the Spirit of the Lord, ***"God is about to over throw the church, but a remnant will arise and obey him. There will be two worlds operating in America. One that is obedient to God that will prosper because God will transfer all the wealth to them. They will run God's Kingdom on earth as it is in Heaven. "Oh, and they won't care about tax breaks and tax loop holes. They will render to Caesar that which is rightfully Caesar's and under gird the financial health of America. Some would*** *argue that the tax breaks are legal; I'd say, "So is abortion!" Both are against God's Kingdom of operation. So, even to obey such in America means to live in the curse and not the Blessing. Remember Joseph in Egypt's famine. God gave him a tax plan that was designed to bring wealth to the country. This is where America missed it. Without taxes; the country cannot survive."*

What about the other world that will be operating in America?

"They will continue to live like they do, but the money will be scarce. They will not live in prosperity, but in lack and in fear for their future. There will be more violence, and hatred as they fight for the meager resources." "Men will become lover's of self, covenant breakers, disobedient . . . Most of those suffering will go to God's Kingdom for relief. The others hate God so much that they will war against God and lose their lives."

How long will these two worlds operate on the earth?

"Until Jesus returns. What's established under God's Kingdom mandate will never be destroyed; even in a country where violence will increase. God's Kingdom will remain. But many will die offended that peace and prosperity will only be in God's Kingdom. The invitation to come to God will be extended, but instead, they will try to tear down the Kingdom and its dwellers. Evil will increase, but so will prosperity" says the Spirit of Grace and Peace.

When can we expect Jesus to return to earth?

The Bible tells us that only God knows the times and season concerning his Kingdom. We do know that Jesus will return to take his church out of the earth before the final disaster occurs. Once the church is removed, there will be only evil and darkness remaining on the earth. Then one final battle ends it all. At that time, Jesus will come back with his mighty army from Heaven and slay the remaining forces of darkness and take possession of the earth. The Book of Revelation tells us much about what to expect during those final days. How many years before Jesus' return, I don't know. But, I do know that I have been commanded to continue my assignment to until he returns. My assignment is just beginning and I have plans on paper through the year 2061. That's forty-two years from now. This is what God gave me. Does that mean that Jesus is coming back in 2061? No! God just gave me a fifty-year plan for the business he wants me to continue until Jesus returns. The point to be made it this. When the systems of the world fail and violence is all around us, most Christians will be looking for Jesus to take them out of here, but it won't happen like that. We are called to *"Occupy til he comes."* So, whenever Jesus does come to earth, he should find his people busy doing Kingdom business. If he comes in fifty, or one hundred years from now, our job is to continue working until he comes.

If God's Kingdom Age is a takeover, how will God deal with those who oppose his will? God is a sovereign power who will deal with his enemies any way he chooses. If you want to get a glimpse of what he might do, read through the Book of Acts. Specifically, the Lord has shown me is that God's enemies may become blind, not able to speak, struck down with heart attacks and deadly illnesses. Some people will even drop dead in public. In other words, the fear of God is about to return to America.

Who does God consider an enemy of his Kingdom? Anyone who speaks against what God's Kingdom could be considered an enemy. For sure those who oppose God's will without repentance are enemies, as are those who plot, scheme and attempt to manipulate their will to masquerade as God's will. God is in the process of removing all who stand in the way of those desiring to enter God's Kingdom. That is why he is overthrowing the portion of the church that is blocking the path to God. Does Kingdom rule mean that God has rejected the church? No! God forbid! God has chosen a remnant by his grace. This is His Church on earth. In Romans Chapter 11, the Apostle Paul explained that not all of Israel would be saved but God had a remnant that would fulfill the covenant. Well, the same will happen to the Christian church. Not all will be saved because like the Jews of old, many in the church have rejected Jesus Christ as their Lord and Master. To fulfill covenant with the Jews and Christians God has no choice but to raise up an obedient remnant that will reach the world with the message of His Kingdom.

Who is the remnant that God will be using? In a vision, the Lord showed me the faces of many he is calling out of Egypt (the world) during this season. They are coming from Hollywood, from the gay community, from street gangs, from government and the market place. These leaders will hear the Kingdom message and eagerly obey God's plan of action. As I saw theses new spiritual leaders, I realized that God was raising up everyone that the church despises; those whom the church has cursed and counted not worthy for the Kingdom. The church would also like to depose Barack Obama, but he is a key player in God's plan. The church's issue with the president is racial, and the Lord is about ***to add insult to injury*** by bringing forth even more minority leaders. God is choosing all of these leaders according to his sovereign will. This is God's justice for our nation's long history of racism and bigotry that was instigated by the Christian church. The Holy Spirit said that, ***"The publicans and harlots shall go into the Kingdom before the church. The first shall be last, and the last shall be first."***

If God's Kingdom models are used by business or the government isn't that a violation of the establishment clause?

No! We are not advocating establishing a national religion. Remember that **Christianity is not a religion. It is a way of living**. Christians are ambassadors of the Kingdom. America is about to get hit so hard, that they will be looking for anyone with a solution, even God. Any solutions we provide won't require people to join a church or religious organization. In the eyes of God, there is no difference between Jew, Christian or an unbeliever. Jesus is Lord of all and he will richly bless all who call on him. God's Kingdom will supersede all kingdoms on earth and it shall never fail. When people recognize the power of the Kingdom to save them from the dire situations of the earth, they will come to him for help. Everyone who calls upon the Lord shall be saved (Romans 10:12-13).

Does God care about any of our political or legislative choices such as Obamacare?

Of course, God cares about everything that involves the lives of human beings on earth. More importantly, God wants us to care about what matters to him. He wants us to live in divine healing and not need a healthcare bill at all. If Christians believe that Jesus is the healer then why fear Obamacare or its implications concerning abortion? Listen, if the people of God are doing things the Kingdom way, we will put Obamacare out of business due to of lack of use. Also no one would need abortions and neither would gay marriage be an issue. Why? Because the Kingdom would supply whatever is lacking in the lives of the people. They would have no reason to continue looking for the government or other means of sustaining their lives.

It was mentioned in one of the chapters that many Kingdom business would be self-sustaining. What does that mean and how does that work? As author, I have had the pleasure of meeting people who have been given a major vision from God. Many of these people have been told to start businesses whose profits would be for the purpose of funding nonprofit ventures around the world. I also had the pleasure of meeting men of God who were actively planning infra structures for economic growth in their communities. In my particular instance, God took me out of the media and entertainment industry. He wanted to show me how to do things the Kingdom way. In the process of doing so, he gave me numerous books, film, music, television projects that he wanted me to produce. I could spend the rest of my life just producing these projects alone, but then God told me that he wanted me to start a nonprofit organization and prepare to build cities in some of the poorest regions of the world. He also said that as many *vessels* as I could find to invest in for his Kingdom, he (God) would cause wealth to flow through my life. The Lord told me that my first distribution from my nonprofit would be $18 million to support around one hundred causes that God wanted me to begin funding. I now, operate my publishing company and corporation not because I want a profit, but because of the promise God gave me concerning wealth. My job is to create what he tells me to create and he will cause the wealth to flow so that I can support the projects on his agenda.

Since, I'm just starting my corporation, I don't have any great monetary accomplishment yet, but whenever I have obeyed God in the past, he has always delivered on his promise. So, rather than being profit oriented, I am more obedient oriented. I believe Matthew 6:32-33, which says, ***Don't worry about the ordinary things of life; but Seek First the Kingdom of God and all these things will be given to you.*** I have seen this work in all areas of my life while employed by others. It's a different thing when you are the owner and CEO of your own corporation. I thank God for mentors like my pastor Dr. Fredrick K.C. Price III. I remember sitting in Dr. Price's office after a recent missions trip to Europe and I shared only a small portion of God's vision for my life. He shared with me his experience of knowing that God wanted him to begin a teaching ministry on television. People look at him now and think that he has always been successful, but they don't realize that when he began it was tough. He was an innovator in many ways. He shared how stepping out in faith means standing on a vision with you and God alone.

People that could help you won't. Others tell you how it cannot be done. Dr. Price told me to make sure that I was hearing from God. Once I am sure that it was God speaking then, hold on to that vision in obedience until God brings it to pass. It's been several years since that conversation. I am grateful for having had personal observation of his walk of faith during the times I was at Crenshaw Christian Center. The meeting in his office that day sealed my determination to go for the vision, even if no one else would go with me.

Over the years, the Lord has connected me with a network of people who have all stepped out in faith on Kingdom projects that are just as colossal as mine. I am planning on doing a series of video interviews with many of them over the next several months under my newly formed company. We have discussed preliminary ideas. The purpose of the series is to show how God is actively giving solutions to America's problems to ordinary people who want to make a difference. It should prove to be an enlightening and inspirational feature as we share the joys of being chosen by God even while being persecuted.

What drew you to the Kingdom? In America we are always being disqualified for something based upon our race, sex, education, profession experience or lack thereof and status in life. In my field of work it was even worse because you also had to have the "right look" to make it. You also have to endure much criticism to be a performer and people can be quite cruel at times. It was not my choice of careers; but it was where the Lord put me; and I did very well because God chose it for me. I also had good agents, but the Holy Spirit served as my manager, he's the one who told me which jobs to take and what to walk away from. At the point when my career was about to skyrocket even further, the Lord pulled me out of the industry. I had several major contract offers that he made me turn down because he said he had something better waiting for me in Los Angeles. He said he had an *"inheritance"* for me; and the only requirement to obtain this inheritance was faith. In fact, he said that was all that required for anyone to receive. This was amazing to me. For once in my life I was being offered something of great value and the only qualification was faith! In my head it seemed too good to be true, but my heart confirmed that God was telling the truth. So, I went for it without even asking what was involved or what I should expect. The Lord took me on an excursion through the Bible and he kept showing me that from the beginning of the world all he wanted was to find a person, a family, and a nation in whom he could award an inheritance. I had been in church all my life, and never had I heard that God had an inheritance for us on earth. So I took off for LA. Along the way the Lord lured me with something better that awaited me in LA. He said that everything that I had lost would be restored to me. He said that destiny awaited me in Los Angeles. Now, how could I turn down an offer like that? My spirit was leaping inside of my chest, so I knew that this was the path I needed to travel. I did have a concern about where to live and how to live in LA without an income, but when I began making arrangements to go, things just fell in place. My cousin, whom I had not heard from since high school, called me out of the blue and asked me to come stay with her in LA. Then my agent went nuts because I turned down major contracts and took off for LA. They just assumed that I had signed a mega blockbuster offer in LA and I would never be able to work for them again. So, they panicked and had all their clients reproduce my commercials that generated enough residual income for me to live in LA without working for almost a year. This was my first demonstration that the Kingdom of God was for real. Some even tried to condemn me for the assignment God gave me. They believed that God only called you into the pulpit ministry. The Church also teaches sin. God only talked about what I needed to release from my life to receive what he had. He spoke to me about *"integrity."* Not only about being moral and honest, but about being whole in my inner being and no longer divided in my allegiances. The Lord told me that I would one day teach about His Kingdom. He said that the church knew nothing about the Kingdom. They talk about the cross, but not about the transformation or the inheritance that is available beyond the cross. Anyone who believes can qualified to receive. This is what caught my attention about God's Kingdom.

What was the most difficult part of your transformation into the Kingdom way of living? There are several things that come to mind, all of which stem from the violence I experienced in my marriage. When God stepped into my life, he told me I had to give up my gun. This was difficult because my .38-caliber pistol was my security. In those days my gun was also the peacekeeper in my marriage. It was well known that if I picked up the gun, I intended to use it, and if I used it, I wasn't going to miss. When God told me to give up my only security, it was painful, but he offered me a better way of protecting myself. He told me that he would teach me how to protect myself by using his word. He also said that my protection was in my obedience. He promised that if I obeyed his instructions, my safety and that of my son would be sure. On the surface, obeying God seemed easy, but because I had been hurt so severely, it was hard for me to trust people. God stepped in by asking if I trusted him. Of course I said yes. Then Lord said that if I trusted him for my life, then I had to trust him to be able to work through other people as it related to my life. Okay, this was plain enough to understand. If God is all-powerful it stands to reason that he could move people to do his will. That's what he was doing with me. The most difficult time was in dealing with family and friends who were Christians, but who could not understand that God requires us to live by faith and not like the rest of the world. I was constantly being told that I should just be like everyone else. That was clearly against what the Spirit of God was leading me to do. When my son was kidnapped by his dad, people criticized me and called me a bad mother. They had no idea of how painful it was to obey God in that situation. No one around me was sympathetic, so it was me and God standing alone.

What kept me faithful to God was his promise of keeping my son and me safe. I could not afford to let others sway me in their direction. For the sake of my life and that of my son, I obeyed God even though the criticism lingers till this day. I had to learn to value God's promise above the opinions of others. Today, I could care less about what people think. I know that the Kingdom works and there's no turning back for me!

You said that God promised to teach you how to protect yourself by using his word. What did you learn? There is not enough time nor space in this book to cover what God taught me, but I will give the overall principle. We mentioned the Law of Seedtime and Harvest. What I learned is that everything that exists on earth (whether bad or good) began with a spiritual seed. This is an easy concept to understand when it comes to appreciating art, design, music or a book. Ideas come from the spirit realm through the human mind. Spiritual seeds come from the realm of the spirit. Their source is either from the Creator God, who has made all things for his pleasure (good), or from the spiritual realm of darkness (evil). These are the only two spiritual realms that influence mankind on earth. Ephesians 6:12 says that we don't war against people, but against spiritual beings in heavenly places. The only seed that will destroy an evil spirit is the word of God (good seed). In my life, the Spirit of God has always given me a *rhema* word to speak over an evil situation. A *rhema* word is something that God speaks directly to your spirit. This is the sword of the Spirit, which is supernaturally designed to cut down the enemy and his weapons. In fact, *The War Journal (1999-2010) Volume I* contains my prayer journal of the battles I won over the enemy. In that book I talk about the issues I faced, and the rhema word God gave me that resulted in a solution. *The War Journal (1999-2010) Volume II* focuses on issues of the church and its effect on America. It also includes rhema word (prophecy) from God about what we need to do to change the situation in our nation. Both books are great examples of what God has taught me about protecting my family, the nation and myself by using his word. God has solutions for every human issue, we need only Ask, Seek and Find out what he has to say.

How can Christians prepare to live in the Kingdom even now?

We must constantly pray **Thy Kingdom Come, Thy Will be done on Earth as it is in Heaven,** and be prepared to do whatever is required of us to get it done. We must praise and worship God alone. We also need to walk by faith and not by fear of political or social movement and their retaliation. Christian leaders talk about politics and "ism" to evoke fear. It doesn't matter if it is communism or socialism. We are called to live by faith. Faith comes by hearing the word of God. God and his word must be exalted above all the "isms" of this world. We exalt whatever we speak the most about. Church leaders have exalted socialism, humanism, atheism, gay marriage-ism, abortion-ism and economy-ism as if they have power over God. When we speak about issues we give them power over our lives. We walk by faith, not by fear. Faith requires that we speak what God tells us to speak and do what God tells us to do. We need to magnify God who has the solutions, and not magnify the problems themselves.

Just by seeing things from a Kingdom perspective, one can greatly improve conditions in the lives of people around the world. Our job should be to speak of nothing except what Jesus Christ has accomplished in his death and resurrection; which is the power to change the world. The same power that raised Jesus from the dead resides inside the heart of every believer; and he (the Holy Spirit) will do exceedingly abundantly above all we could ever ask or think according to how much we allow his power to work through us (Ephesians 3:20). Need more power in your life? Trust God instead of the government or even your circumstances. Obey God and the Holy Spirit will take it from there.

Congratulations!

You Have Successfully Completed

AMERICAN HERITAGE 101

BIBLIOGRAPHY

Copeland, Kenneth; Roberts, Oral; Roberts, Richard. *The Wake-Up Call*. Fort Worth: Kenneth Copeland Publications, 2004.

Matthews, Paula. *The War Journal (1999-2010) Volume I*. Los Angeles: Spirit & Life Publications, 2010.

Matthews, Paula. *The War Journal (1999-2010) Volume II*. Los Angeles: Spirit & Life Publications, 2011.

The Holy Bible: Authorized King James Version. Nashville: Thomas Nelson, 2003.

ENDNOTES

1 "Mayflower Compact." MayflowerHistory.com, mayflowerhistory.com/mayflower-compact.

2 Jefferson, et al. "Religion and the Founding of the American Republic Religion and the Federal Government, Part 2." Planning D-Day (April 2003) - Library of Congress Information Bulletin, Victor, 4 June 1998, www.loc.gov/exhibits/religion/rel06-2.html.

3 Akaka, and Daniel K. "S.J.Res.19 - 103rd Congress (1993-1994): A Joint Resolution to Acknowledge the 100th Anniversary of the January 17, 1893 Overthrow of the Kingdom of Hawaii, and to Offer an Apology to Native Hawaiians on Behalf of the United States for the Overthrow of the Kingdom of Hawaii." Congress.gov, 23 Nov. 1993, www.congress.gov/bill/103rd-congress/senate-joint-resolution/19.

4 Matteson, et al. "Religion and the Founding of the American Republic Religion and the Congress of the Confederation." Planning D-Day (April 2003) - Library of Congress Information Bulletin, Victor, 4 June 1998, www.loc.gov/exhibits/religion/rel04.html.

www.ingramcontent.com/pod-product-compliance
Lightning Source LLC
Chambersburg PA
CBHW042310150426
43198CB00001B/26